Dana O.

Surviving Your Adolescents

How to Manage *and Let Go Of*
Your 13 to 18 Year Olds

Surviving Your Adolescents

Thomas W. Phelan, Ph.D.

CHILD MANAGEMENT INC
Glen Ellyn, Illinois

Cover design and illustrations by Margaret Mayer
Cover copy by Brett Jay Markel
Cover photography by Steve Orlick
Child Management Logo by Steve Roe

Distributed by Login Publishers Consortium

Printed in the United States of America
10 9 8 7 6 5 4 3 2 1

For more information, contact:
Child Management, Inc.
800 Roosevelt Road
Glen Ellyn, Illinois 60137

Publisher's Cataloging in Publication
(Prepared by Quality Books Inc.)

Phelan, Thomas W., 1943-
   Surviving your adolescents: how to manage and let go of your 13 to 18 year olds/Thomas W. Phelan.
   p. cm.
   ISBN 0-9633861-0-7

   1. Parenting. 2. Child rearing. 3. Parent and child. 4. Teenagers.   I. Title.

HQ755.P44 1993   649.125
                                                  QB193-969

To the "kids,"

Tom and Julie

Contents

Part IV: No Teenager Will Thank You

Part V: Managing Specific Problems

Part VI: The Future

Introduction

L iving with a teenager is no picnic. There are times when you must bite your tongue as they push towards independence. After all, they're not supposed to live with you forever. There are also times, though, when you must intervene if you sense there is trouble.

A parent, therefore, needs to know when to be quiet and when to act. They also need to know *what to do* when something needs to be done. All this comes on top of the often perplexing job of simply getting along with the adolescent in the first place!

Surviving Your Adolescents is a kind of practical guidebook for parents of adolescents in approximately the thirteen to eighteen year old age bracket. It offers guidelines for handling the complex situations and dilemmas that teenagers often present. It is intended to be concrete and down-to-earth, offering specific suggestions—many of which can be applied immediately.

This book is, in a sense, a follow-up to the *1-2-3 Magic: Training Your Children to Do What You Want* also produced by Child Management, Inc. Many of the basic principles are similar, such as the No-Talking and No-Emotion Rules, and to derive maximum benefit, parents may want

1

to read *1-2-3 Magic* as well. Adolescents, however, require quite different treatment in many ways than their younger counterparts, so you will find many new suggestions. Both books see parenting on a continuum from taking charge to letting go. The younger the children, the more parents need to take charge; the older they are, the more parents need to get used to letting go.

Surviving Your Adolescents also tries to recognize the fact that parents—especially parents of adolescents—do not possess infinite quantities of the following things:

> *Time*
> *Energy*
> *Skill*
> *Patience*

Parents of teens have many problems to juggle in their lives. Many work full or part-time. They also have to keep up the house, worry about their own aging parents, stay healthy, and keep their spouses happy. And how about getting the car over for that new muffler?

With all this going on, parents don't need a parenting manual that is complicated, time consuming, and perhaps guilt inducing. They do need something that is straightforward, practical, and that offers some specific "how to" advice.

Surviving Your Adolescents attempts to provide just that. Part I opens by providing an orientation to adolescence in general. Teens and their parents are not from the same planet, and it is essential to know how they are different. Each parent is then encouraged to objectively evaluate their own situation, and many mothers and fathers have found a good deal of relief in just doing that. Some problems may be aggravating but not serious. Others may require professional attention.

Next we turn our attention, in Part II, to simply getting along. Parents need to keep an eye on their own state of mind and their own welfare if they are to interact positively with their kids and avoid the emotional dumping that can lead to a State of War. They must avoid at all costs the "Four Cardinal Sins." Then, if they have the time and energy left, some interesting suggestions are made for maintaining or improving a relationship with a teenage son or daughter. Some can be done immediately, but none of them is easy.

Part III suggests four possible roles that parents can consider when they are concerned about something. They vary from doing nothing (Observer) to taking charge (Director), and it is important that a parent match the role to the problem. Teenagers do not take kindly to unnecessary interventions!

Neither will they thank you when you do have to do something assertive in their interests. So Part IV examines the Six Kinds of Testing and Manipulation and provides clear recommendations for how to handle them.

Part V suggests some concrete ideas for managing some of the most common problems that adolescents present to their parents. It also gives some specific examples of how to apply the principles and methods discussed earlier in the book. The list of problems includes:

Arguing	Music
Bedtime	Meals & eating habits
Bumming around town	Messy rooms
Car: care, use, gas	Money, allowance, loans
Chores	Negative attitude
Church	Parties: home & away
Clothes, hair, earrings	Phone
College plans	Sex
Depression	Sibling rivalry
Drugs & drinking	Smoking cigarettes
Family outings	Swearing
Friends & dating	Behavioral trouble at school
Grades	Using your things
Grammar	Vacations
Homework	Work
Hours	

Finally, Part VI attempts to take a look at the future. Did you every stop to think that an eighteen year old is just twelve years away from being thirty? That may sound like an eternity right now, but for most of us, those years sped by all too quickly.

This book is not intended to be a replacement for counseling or psychotherapy when that is indicated. Chapter 12 clearly defines problems for which a professional evaluation is necessary. In fact, many people have found that the ideas in *Surviving Your Adolescents* are often very helpful when they are integrated into psychological treatment, especially since these ideas do not require the parent to be a genius, saint, or professional psychotherapist in order to apply them.

As with *1-2-3 Magic*, the methods presented here are also based upon the actual experiences of parents, as well as the author's own parenting and clinical work. A very large number of these parents had to deal with Attention Deficit Disorder children, one of the hardest groups there is to manage. The techniques described here, therefore, are quite practical and down-to-earth. ADD kids don't give you much room to monkey around, and there is a lot of truth to the statement, "If you can handle an ADD child, you can handle anybody!"

Parent of adolescent: there is no magical cure for this difficult condition. It is, however, short-lived. We hope that *Surviving Your Adolescents* will help you—and your teenagers—live through it as pleasantly as possible.

Part I

Thinking Straight

Realistic Thinking

B efore we take a look at how you as a parent can deal with the
different problems that teens can present to themselves and
to you, we need to get some overall picture of the general "mental status"
of teenagers as well as the mental status of their parents. Where are these
people likely to be at this point in their lives? Unfortunately, when you
examine the situation closely, you may be more impressed by the *differences* between the kids and their parents than by the similarities.

Adolescents differ from their parents in three fundamental ways, and
it is important to keep these in mind before trying to handle problems.
You and your child may not inhabit the same world.

Difference 1

Teens: More Dreams than Realities

The teenage years are a time of great excitement and great turmoil. The
excitement comes from what often feels to the child like the unlimited
possibilities ahead. The mind of the adolescent, therefore, is occupied
with *more dreams than realities*. The dreams are endless and in a sense—

they can *all* be had at the same time in one's fantasies. On the other hand, the dreams are not realities yet, and this yields an often painful sense of inferiority and lack of identity. The career that may come does not exist and may not even be chosen; the family (spouse and kids) one may create later is not around *now*.

The result is that adolescents spend a lot of time in fantasy. Their whole life is before them, and they like to dream about what it will be like. The psychological pain that may result from the current lack of fulfillment can easily be dealt with by such daydreaming. Teens also have not had a lot of experience yet in testing these dreams out against reality, so many of their notions may seem crazy to their parents. Where are their parents?

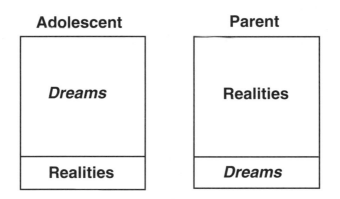

Parents: More Realities than Dreams

Midlife! The notion strikes terror into the hearts of some people. If parents are old enough to have teenage sons and daughters, they are old enough to be at this difficult point in their own lives. It is for many a point which involves the painful realization that there are now *more realities than dreams*, and the realities are certainly not all that they were once cracked up to be.

The career that once held such great promise may not have produced the desired financial rewards, status, or satisfaction. Even for those who are successful, each morning demands getting out of bed for a repeat performance. Others feel a vague longing after 15-20 years on a job for something different.

Of all the cherished dreams of childhood and adolescence, perhaps the one that takes the greatest beating with the passage of time involves love and marriage. In recent years the divorce rate has hovered around 50%, though it may be decreasing some now. Even some couples that remain together may do so for reasons of finances, children, life style, and so on--even if they are not especially happy with their relationship with their spouse. It therefore appears that the odds of experiencing a satisfying marriage may be substantially better than 50% against you, a far cry from the "they lived happily ever after" feeling many people had on the day they got married.

As if this weren't enough stress, midlife also brings with it increasing health problems and a greater consciousness that life won't last forever, or what one writer called a sense of "the dark at the end of the tunnel." Many of the parents' own parents may have died already, making these realities more graphic.

For some people these thoughts are not always conscious, but lurk off and on in the back of their minds. But the awareness, for example, that you are now older—rather than younger—than almost all of the major league baseball players, or that many of your favorite childhood actors, actresses, and singers are dead, can give you the uneasy feeling that life is more than half over. This certainly does not mean that all these parents are depressed, but it does mean that they will be experiencing stresses that are regular and predictable.

Difference 2

Independence Is Their Big Task

By the time the kids are 13-18, their folks' job of raising them is 60-80% over. Many parents fail to realize this. Their teens, however, may be trying to act like the job were 100% over! Even though they can get a little pushy about this sometimes, one of their main jobs during adolescence *is* to begin to establish their independence. You don't, after all, want them to stay home forever. Therefore, one of your main jobs as a parent is to gradually pull back or *let go*, slowly giving them more and more say in their own affairs.

"Letting Go" Is Your Big Task

When are they ready to handle things themselves? This is not an easy question to answer. Even though they may be biologically ready to do many of the things adults can, a technologically oriented industrial and service type of society such as ours imposes long delays on its youngsters so they can be educated. To the teens, however, this education sometimes feels too much like mere babysitting, and for many kids the forced wait produces feelings of frustration and rebellion. Meanwhile their parents are agonizing over whether or not their children are ready to handle problems from dating, driving, and money to drinking and sex.

Part of the result of this is that *teens have to be different!* Of all the creatures on earth the human animal has the longest period of dependence upon its parents, and for the teens this is often just plain insulting. Therefore they will search for ways—which their parents sometimes feel are ridiculous—to differentiate themselves, prove they can handle life, and show some signs of competence and independence. This may involve anything from a job to an earring! You, though, would probably prefer that they try to emphasize the similarities they share with you.

"When I was a kid..."

Difference 3

They Invest in Peers

Complicating the picture for the adolescent is the fact that this time in their lives involves probably the greatest social sensitivity they will ever feel. Whom they know, who likes them, and whom they hang around with are extremely important. Part of the reason that many teens are so negative about the notions of "popularity" and "status" is that they feel these needs so deeply. But don't try to tell them that unless you want to fight.

You Invest in Them

The intensity of these social needs also dictates that the child begin to pull away from Mom, Dad, and family and establish their own social network outside the home. This is not always accomplished smoothly or with great tact. Parents will often be hurt or angered when a teenager declines an invitation to go out with them, or when they find out that their child doesn't consider it to be too neat to be seen in public with their mother or father.

Adolescents, however, are supposed to be establishing relationships with peers and beginning to pull away from home. Even though you may not always agree with their choice of friends, their ultimate goal is to be able to live independently, set up their own family, and maintain a satisfying social life for themselves. This is really what you—as their parent—would want for them too.

Dreamer Meets Disillusioned

What happens when Dreamer meets Disillusioned? It's hard to imagine a worse combination! These people are supposed to talk over problems and get somewhere? Many adolescents and their parents get along very well, of course, but there are still some frequent and common problems that parents can run into when their children reach the ages of 13 to 18. Here are some of the more usual ones:

Old "tapes"

Parents were once adolescents themselves, believe it or not. Most people have fairly vivid memories of what their teen years were like, and when their children reach the same stage of life, Mom and Dad often find that their children's experiences trigger old "tapes" of some of their past successes and conflicts. This sometimes results in overidentification with the teen's problems, producing a lot of "what if" thoughts and anxiety about possible disasters. An overly anxious parent will invariably aggravate a teenager, and this can produce arguments, misunderstandings, and a tremendous amount of domestic conflict.

On the other hand, based on their past experiences, many parents cannot identify with their teen, and this produces anger. Mom and Dad get irritated with their child because they cannot understand the thinking and feelings behind the teens's actions, and so often they attempt to overcontrol the adolescent, which can also, unfortunately, result in much turmoil.

Sometimes it seems you just can't win.

Reflections

Most parents inevitably see their children as a reflection on themselves. It is certainly no fun to feel that your self-esteem is in the hands of someone else. Children *are* a reflection on their parents to some extent, but this feeling is often overdone, and the parents' fear of embarrassment can sometimes get so strong that it again leads to attempts at overcontrol. It may help Mom and Dad to realize that their children never were putty in their hands, and that they were affected by many other influences in growing up, such as heredity, friends, society, good and bad luck, other adults, and so on.

Crash courses

If the parenting job is mostly over, it's definitely getting late. Some parents, looking at their 17 year old son, for example, don't like what they see and are tempted to get into "crash courses"—last ditch attempts to get the kid to shape up. This often involves attempts at "insight transplants" via long lectures, scoldings, or arguments, and, of course, these are rarely successful. It's almost as if we parents see ourselves as manufacturers of some kind. The child is our product. He's getting close to the end of the assembly line, but he's not what he's supposed to be. Better get in there quick and do something!

Parental power

Do I still have any power as a parent? It's certainly easy to feel helpless sometimes in dealing with an adolescent. In some areas you *are* helpless—and even should be—but don't lose heart: there is still some power there when you need it. Later we will define exactly what kinds of leverage you still do have, but it must be used judiciously—not impulsively.

2

Sizing Up Your Situation

Being objective in thinking about a teen is very difficult. Then again, it's not so easy being objective about yourself either. Many people in our culture suffer from self-esteem problems because they don't know how to evaluate themselves properly. In a moment we're going to ask you to evaluate both your teenager and yourself, but first we need to provide a short course in straight thinking. Otherwise you may begin this whole program on the wrong foot.

In a moment we'll ask you to evaluate three aspects of your current situation: your teen, your relationship with them, and, finally, how you are doing yourself. Why should we bother to do this? There are very good reasons.

First of all, *it's easy to focus on one or two problems* so much that you lose your perspective on your child. Evaluating "your" adolescent objectively may help you relax. Second, if you rate your relationship with your son or daughter as pretty bad, *you may be the last person in the world who should try to talk to them about a problem.* And third, if you feel you yourself are not doing so well, trying to deal with a teen's problems *may simply result in you dumping a lot of hostile emotion* on them.

Objectivity: The "9 & 1" Rule

If you do 10 things in the course of a day, 9 of them right and 1 wrong, which do you think about at the end of the day?

Of course, the one you goofed up! That seems reasonable enough, doesn't it? Some people take this line of thinking further and come to the conclusion that because of this performance they must be an idiot or a jerk.

This is not fair, but it's a very common way of thinking. What the person does here is base his opinion of himself on only a small portion of his overall behavior. Some people refer to this as "overgeneralization," otherwise known as making a mountain out of a molehill. But the fact of the matter is that most of us are much more impressed by the things that we do wrong than by the things that we do right. There is probably some biological base to this which may have its foundations in evolutionary theory. Wouldn't it be nice to have a species of animal that was continually problem focused and always on the lookout, and that never just sat around wasting time feeling good about what it had accomplished?

Maybe. That species would certainly be very durable and adaptable. But you might not want to be a member of it! You would always be torturing yourself about everything you are not doing right, while you continually take for granted everything you *do* do right. Since you could never be perfect, you would thus be set up for a life of mental self-abuse.

This is exactly what many—or perhaps most—human beings do. If they do 9 of 10 things correctly, they abuse themselves about the 1 they did wrong. They conclude that they are idiots.

Let's turn the situation around, but use the same logic. Imagine a day where you do 10 different things, 9 of them wrong and 1 right, and that evening you come to the conclusion that you are Superwoman or Superman. Doesn't that seem rather dumb? Most people, oddly enough, will agree that that doesn't make sense, but they have a much harder time seeing the illogic in concluding that they are incompetent when only a small portion of their actions were faulty.

The conclusion? Your self-esteem should be based upon a realistic perception of yourself. If, in fact, you are doing most of what you should reasonably well, if most of what you are doing is constructive (including having fun!), and if in general you are taking care of business and getting along with most people, you probably qualify as a basically decent and competent person. Your self-esteem—if you are realistic—should not crumble if you are not perfect or if you are not doing something that is special or unique.

Part of the reason for going into this issue here is this: *if you evaluate yourself unfairly using unrealistic rules, you will also tend to evaluate other family members unfairly.* If you apply the standards of perfectionism and overgeneralization to your teens, you will be much more impressed, angered, hurt, etc., by their bad behavior and tend to take for granted their good behavior—which for most kids is 90% of what they do. When we ask you in just a moment to evaluate your son or daughter, try to keep this in mind.

Before you think about handling (or not handling) a problem with a teen, you will need to objectively answer the following questions:

A. *What sort of teen do you have?*
B. *What sort of relationship do you have with them?*
C. *How are you doing yourself now?*

The answers to these questions will often help you decide what kind of approach to take with your teenager regarding a particular problem, or whether or not you need to do anything at all. If both parents are living at home and you are reading this book with your spouse, do the ratings separately, then compare them later. The differences between you can be very important.

A. What Child Is This?

Taking everything into account, how is your adolescent doing with his or her life right now? It is admittedly difficult and oversimplified to give your child an overall rating or grade for this, but the idea does have some validity and you are doing it all the time anyway. Comments like "She's a great kid," "I can't stand that jerk," and "You'd better get your act together," all reflect our tendency to generalize about our children.

So if you're going to generalize (not *over*generalize) about your son or daughter, let's try to do it as reasonably and objectively as possible. While keeping in mind the "9 & 1" Rule, think of five main areas: Home, Social Life, School, Work (if applicable), and Self-esteem. Give your child an overall rating for all the areas put together, using the following scale:

Competent (5)

Pretty good (4)

Average or OK (3)

Poor (2)

Problem child (1)

The Competent child (rated "5"), for example, gets along well with family and presents few discipline problems, has close friends as well as acquaintances, enjoys school and is working up to capacity, is responsible at work and rated well by his or her supervisor, and feels reasonably OK about himself (keep in mind that the self-esteem of an adolescent should be a little bit shaky).

The Average teen ("3") gets along well in the family mostly but can present significant problems and turmoil at times. They have some friends, though you may not always care for them. The child feels so-so about school and academically operates at—or a little below—his capacity. If he has a job, he works off and on, is fairly reliable, and has occasional minor problems with supervisors. The teen has times when he feels he's not so hot (whether or not this is said out loud), but does not seem to be overly self-critical most of the time.

The Problem child (rated "1") is distant, hostile, and often argumentative at home; you may love him but have difficulty liking him. He is a loner or hangs out with kids you dislike intensely and who you feel are bad influences on him. He hates school and works well below his overall intellectual ability. He either doesn't work, gets fired or quits a lot, and has trouble with supervision. Though defensive and never prone to graciously taking negative feedback, he obviously has a poor self image.

If a child is good in one area and poor in another, you may "average" them as best you can. Remember this evaluation is not perfect, and the result will be some combination of subjectivity and objectivity. But it is very important to take a long, hard, realistic look at your offspring, rather than thinking impulsively and then shooting from the hip when it comes to some kind of problem solving. Is your child really as bad as you have been thinking? Are there problems primarily just in one area or are there many areas of concern? Which areas are the adolescent's strengths? Are problems worse than you thought and have you been denying their existence or severity?

B. How Do the Two of You Get Along?

This time look at how well you and your adolescent get along. Think here of three dimensions: *Talking Together, Shared Fun, and Liking* (not loving). Use the following rating system:

> *Good relationship (5)*
> *Get along pretty well (4)*
> *Average relationship (3)*
> *Not so hot (2)*
> *Bad relationship (1)*

In a relationship rated "5," you and your teen get along extremely well. You can discuss and resolve problems as well as enjoy just "shooting the breeze"—spontaneously spending time together just talking about whatever comes to mind. You often do enjoyable things together, and don't have a lot of trouble finding things that you *both* can enjoy. You genuinely like (and love) one another, and look forward to the other person's company.

In an average, or "3," relationship you talk sometimes, but it's sometimes awkward or hostile. Occasionally you will find yourselves talking spontaneously about some interesting subject. Problems are sometimes resolved when you discuss them, but these discussions can also lead to arguments and no resolution. You do a few things together from time to time, but your interests vary and you often can't understand why the other person likes what they do. You find each other pleasant to be with at times, but you also can find one another taxing and irritating.

The bottom of the barrel in relationships here will receive a rating of

"1." Things between the two of you are consistently terrible. You never talk, or if you try to you just argue. You tend to take opposite sides on even neutral topics. Aggravating problems are not resolved and just continue to simmer. You don't do anything together and generally consider the other person's interests idiotic. Though you may still love one another, you basically find the other person obnoxious.

Keep in mind, while making this rating, that you are *not* comparing your relationship to what it was before, because it is normal for the child to be pulling away from their family and from you at this time.

C. How Are You Doing?

How well you handle the normal irritations as well as the bigger problems you encounter with an adolescent can depend a lot on how well you are doing. Now evaluate yourself at this point in time, which should be approximately midlife for you. Think of three dimensions: Daily Stress, Usual Mood, and Self-esteem. We'll call this your "General Stress Index" (GSI):

Life is great (5)
Things are pretty good (4)
I'm doing OK (3)
Things are not so hot (2)
Life is awful (1)

If you gave yourself a GSI of "5," you feel happy most of the time and generally satisfied with things (no one is happy *all* the time). Your job and relationships with your spouse and important other people can provide stress, but you normally find your activities more rewarding and the stress you feel is usually challenging and nothing you can't handle. You have fun on a regular basis. Even though you know you're not perfect, you know that basically you're a pretty decent, competent, and nice person, and that other people also appreciate this about you.

The parent rating themselves with a "3" feels that life is OK to so-so. Sometimes they feel fine and sometimes not so good. They experience a fair amount of stress and sometimes are not so sure how to handle it. They can occasionally have fun, and it may include doing things with other people. Their perception of themselves is that they're about average, and they may also be aware of significant weaknesses in their behavior or personality that bother them.

A GSI of "1" here means that life is the pits. You usually feel down and/or burned out. Problems that you have are generally overwhelming and you don't feel at all capable of handling them. You don't have a lot of fun and tend to avoid spending much time with other people. Your self-esteem is nonexistent. Often you see yourself as being nobody, totally useless, or a jerk. Or all of the above.

Once again, in making these ratings try to think as objectively as possible. Often middle aged people, when thinking about age and aging, tend to go to extremes. They either kid around all the time or get excessively morbid. What is the reality of your life right now?

Snapshots: Possible Combinations

If we put the three ratings together (Teen, Relationship, Self), we get a sort of "snapshot" of the present situation and, hopefully, some kind of perspective on what's currently going on. There are, of course, many possible combinations. A "5-5-5" (child rated 5, relationship rated 5, and parent rated 5), for example, would obviously be the best. A "3-3-3" would be average, and "1-1-1" the worst.

Things don't always come out so neatly, of course. Here are some examples of situations that are somewhat unusual, but which definitely can occur. Try to figure out what might be going on if you were experiencing the following scenarios:

5-5-1: Here the child is doing just fine and the relationship with the parent is very good, but the parent is doing lousy. The adolescent may be providing a good deal of support to this troubled parent, but does not need much help or intervention in return.

1-5-5: The adolescent is a disaster area, but the relationship with the parent is very good and the parent is doing very well. Would a parent rate themselves a 5 if the child were doing so poorly? Maybe not, but if the ratings are accurate, this parent is in an excellent position to help the troubled child, but the problems are many and the parent may need help—

from the other spouse and perhaps from professional counseling as well.

1-5-1: This one doesn't make a lot of sense, but it has happened. The parent and teenager are both doing poorly, but they get along very well. Better check three things here: do the two get along based on something that is abnormal, pathological, and really not good for either of them? How do the two parents get along with each other? Chances are the marriage is in trouble.

5-5-5: Why are you reading this book?

5-1-5: This situation may seem unlikely, but it is not as uncommon as you would think. The adolescent is doing fine, the parent is doing fine, but their relationship stinks! Best bet: stay out of each other's way, and if there are problems, hope the other spouse (if both parents are living at home) can pick up the slack. Why is the relationship so bad? One possibility is that both child and parent—for some reason—have a real problem using the "9 & 1" Rule when thinking about each other.

1-1-1: You may use this book for a starter course, but much more will be needed. Dealing with any problem will be extremely difficult—if not impossible—whether the problem is brushing teeth (which you probably shouldn't be involved in anyway) or grades.

3-3-3: Hold your breath. Things are going along OK for the most part, and in the long run chances are everything will be fine. But if you're worried about things not continuing as they are, see what you can do to take care of yourself and avoid the Four Cardinal Sins like the plague. Then, if you have the energy and time, check out some of the strategies for improving a relationship.

1-3-5: Sounds like most people's golf score. The teen is doing badly, the relationship is so-so, and the parent is doing very well. Here the parent should think about working on the relationship first—unless there is some kind of emergency—and then deal with problems one at a time. If it hasn't already been done, professional assistance might be a good idea

5-2-1: Leave the kid alone. Don't use him for target practice because you are having a terrible time of it.

1-3-1: The child's doing terribly, but so are you. You are in no position to deal with a troublesome adolescent right now. Better see if there's help from your spouse or get some professional advice.

One More Thing: The State of the Union

There's one other important area we haven't evaluated: the current status of the marriage. It certainly isn't new anymore. The relationship may still be basically good, it may be going along reasonably well, or it may be very conflictual. These different possibilities obviously have implications for dealing with teenagers, with the last one offering the adolescent many opportunities for "playing both ends against the middle."

There may also already have been a divorce or even a death, and as a result you may have what is often euphemistically called a "blended family." Teenagers are much harder to "blend" than younger children, because they don't attach or "bond" to stepparents as well as younger kids.

You don't have to rate or grade the marriage here, but think for a moment what effect it has on the teen. Some parents fight like cats and dogs, but when it comes to the kids, they agree perfectly! Some couples fight like cats and dogs *about the kids*. Some couples don't fight out loud, but you can cut the tension in the house with a knife. Also, don't forget that children can hear through walls and heating ducts all too easily, and they often remember hearing arguments—especially those that were about them.

A good general rule of thumb is this: if you are going to argue in front of the kids, resolve it in front of the kids—quickly. Otherwise don't argue in front of them; go off to a separate room and see if you can solve the problem and agree on something. Then come back and present your position to the children.

At this point you should have a somewhat better perspective on what is going on at your house. Before going on to what to do about your concerns, let's take a quick look at how serious different problems with teenagers can be.

How Serious Is It?

Take just a minute to make sure you have your perspective on something else: how serious are the different types of problems adolescents come up with? If you stop to think about it, it may be that not all problems are created equal.

Your Teens Have Their MBAs!

Many things that adolescents do—or don't do—fall into the "MBA" category. That means they are *Minor But Aggravating*. It's very important for parents to keep in mind that *their level of aggravation about a problem is not always a measure of the seriousness of that problem.* Just because you get ferociously angry about something, in other words, doesn't mean that it is a sign of a major character flaw, mental illness, or sociopathic tendencies in your offspring. It may be just a part of normal adolescence.

What kinds of problems fall into the MBA category? One of the best examples is the use of the phone. Do you know that long, pointless, and apparently stupid conversations between teenagers over the phone are normal and healthy? This is what kids are supposed to be doing at this age, so when they do it this is actually good!

23

The phone rings, for example, and your sixteen year old daughter dives for it. The following conversation ensues:

"Hello."
"Hi. What are you doing?"
"Nothing. What are you doing?"
"Nothing."
"Cool."

Two hours later not much more of significance is being discussed. You start fuming thinking about your phone bill and about how she could spend her time better doing extra credit work for biology.

Cool it. This is good for kids. They are making contact with each other. They are learning how to handle relationships. It's good for their self-esteem. Would you rather they weren't talking to anyone?

If you're concerned about the phone bill, make a deal that they pay for any charges over a certain amount per month. Otherwise, leave them alone and don't listen.

Another MBA type "problem" has to do with dress and appearance. This includes clothing, hair, earrings, and other attachments to the body. It's not reasonable to expect your teens to want to dress like you. Remember, part of their thinking is that they often want to look as *different* from you as possible.

One solution to the appearance problem we've recommended for years is this: let the kids wear anything that the school will let them in the door with. This, of course, isn't saying a lot, because schools' criteria are not too strict these days, but it does offer some control.

Another MBA? That messy room. What a pit! Your stomach writhes in agony every time you look at it. Do you know that there are no studies that prove that teens with messy rooms grow up to be homeless persons, schizophrenics, or have a higher divorce rate than the rest of the population?

What's the solution? It may be to close the door and don't look. Or leave the door open and just close your eyes as you go past. This is aggravating but it isn't a major problem. A messy room is not a sure indicator of deep psychological trouble. Also, be realistic. If all the nagging and arguing and lecturing you've done over the years hasn't convinced your seventeen year old son to clean his room regularly, he isn't going to start now no matter what you do. You have lost the battle, but it's not the end of the world. And you don't want arguing about it to be the end of your relationship.

Other MBAs

Here are some other probable Minor But Aggravating problems that perhaps you should consider letting go of:

Musical preferences	Eating habits
Chores	Grammar
Not going on family outings	Using your things

These can all certainly be aggravating—in fact, *very* aggravating—but they should not necessarily be taken as indications that your child is in deep psychological trouble. Remember that a cardinal rule for parents of adolescents is: Never open your mouth unless you have a very good reason.

On the possible MBA list are things like arguing, bedtime, swearing, and bumming around town. These may or not be more serious depending on your situation. They are obviously less serious the more competent you feel your teenager is. They are also less aggravating the better your relationship with the child is and the better you are doing yourself.

By the way, can you guess which two problems are mentioned *most frequently* by parents? Not drugs and drinking, and not even smoking. In our surveys the "winners" have consistently been arguing and sibling rivalry. This does not, of course, mean they are the most serious.

What Are Not MBAs?

Adolescence is difficult enough for kids and their parents to begin with. But sometimes certain psychological problems—which are definitely not MBAs—are added to the picture. These can often cause intense suffering for the adolescents as well as their parents, and most often parents should *not* try to manage them on their own. Professional evaluation and counseling are essential (see Chapter 12). These more serious, non-MBA problems include the following:

Anxiety Disorders: some children are biologically predisposed to have excessive fears. These anxieties can relate to social situations, separation, obsessive thoughts, and life in general.

Depression: true clinical depression involves a consistently gloomy view of life and, in adolescents, persistent irritability. It lowers self-esteem, takes the joy out of things, and is often accompanied by appetite and sleeping disturbances, social withdrawal, and underachievement.

Attention Deficit Disorder: probably the most common childhood and adolescent problem. The poor concentration skills and frequent intense temperaments of these children can affect all areas of their lives—at school, at home, and with peers.

Conduct Disorder: perhaps a euphemism for what used to be called "juvenile delinquency." CD kids are defiant, abuse the rights of others, and can prematurely get into acting out involving sex, drugs, stealing and fighting. They blame everyone else for their problems.

Eating Disorders: anorexic girls refuse to maintain a normal bodyweight and have very distorted images of their own bodies. Bulimics can maintain a normal weight, but often engage in binge-purge routines that jeopardize their physical health and trigger intense shame.

Alcohol and Drug Abuse: it is common for teens to experiment with alcohol and marijuana. Some, however, overuse these substances or use them in combination on a regular basis. A major problem exists when the drug use becomes a central life activity for the adolescent.

Divorce Related Problems: kids are resilient, but recent evidence suggests that parents' divorce can be especially traumatic for some children. When remarriages are involved, adolescents are harder to merge into the "blended family," causing extreme stress on second marriages.

Sexual Abuse: estimates of the percentage of girls who have been sexually abused vary widely, but there is no doubt the number is high. The effects on a child can range from precocious sexual activity to chronic guilt, poor interpersonal relationships and low self-esteem.

Not all worrisome or irritating things are the same. Perhaps you're having a cow about a relatively minor thing. On the other hand, perhaps you're ignoring a problem with which you need professional assistance.

Part II

Getting Along

4

Taking Care of Yourself

Earlier we asked you how you were doing in terms of daily stress, general mood, and self-esteem. Believe it or not, the first step in getting along with any adolescent is to make sure you're OK. If in Chapter 2 you rated yourself as not doing too well, it might be helpful if you attended to your own problems first. After you get yourself back on track, you can go back to worrying about your child.

Emotional Dumping

If you are not doing well, there are several reasons why taking care of yourself first might be a good idea—or why it may, in fact, be essential. One reason for taking care of yourself first is the fact that if you are really stressed out, you will not be able to talk about any problems without getting very upset. You will just be too sore. You will, therefore, do more damage to your relationships with others, and you will also not be very likely to solve any problems very well.

A second reason for taking care of yourself is quite simple: why should you spend another hour of your life feeling unnecessary pain, if there's something you can do about it?

Finally, if you are in bad shape, perhaps the biggest problem you will experience is one that you may not even be aware of. It is called "displacement." This is kind of a fancy term for what is otherwise known as "emotional dumping." It refers to our uncanny tendency to transfer feelings from one situation to another—without really being aware of what we are doing. A father who has just been chewed out by his boss at work, for example, may return home and yell at his wife because their three year old left her tricycle in the driveway.

The odd thing about this, however, is that while Dad is yelling at his wife, he will actually feel and believe that the bike is the problem. The real source of his being so stressed out—what happened at work—will sort of become "unconscious" to him, or more or less forgotten. His wife, of course, will also believe that the tricycle is the problem, unless she at some point gets more information.

The problem with displacement, therefore, actually involves two things: 1) an exaggeration of the seriousness of a problem, and 2) a focus on the wrong problem. How does this apply to handling a problem with an adolescent? If you are really doing poorly yourself, you will tend to have an exaggerated view of the seriousness of your teen's problems. Everything will seem like a big deal, even though it may not be so bad. You might, for example, think of a kid who really is average or competent as a walking catastrophe. You might also get all upset about minor problems, such as a messy room, or a lot of time spent on the phone.

Perhaps worst of all, you might not realize that the biggest source of your distress is *you*, the midlifer, and not your child. If your teenager has some sense that this is going on—he is basically OK but you are overreacting to minor offenses—he will begin to resent you more and more.

War!

Kids, of course, can dump or displace their negative feelings onto their parents, just as parents can onto the kids. If this goes on for too long—and especially if it's going both ways—it can produce a more or less permanent state of war.

A number of years ago, Eric Berne wrote a book called *Games*

People Play. In it he described some of the rather goofy ways that people can interact with each other, and he labeled these unproductive events "games." A game always had some superficial plausibility to it, according to Berne, but underneath the "player" was really trying to accomplish something else—often some hidden, emotional , and self-serving objective.

Berne always had somewhat odd, humorous titles for his games, such as "Kick Me" and "Why Does This Always Happen to Me!" What is probably the most common of these games, however, he called "Now I've Got You, You Son-of-a-Bitch!" In this game one person repeatedly catches another doing something wrong and then scolds, blasts, or lectures them for their transgression.

The plausible part of the game is that something was done that was wrong, and it might need to be pointed out or corrected. The hidden part of the game, though, is the emotional satisfaction the chief player gets out of venting his spleen and having a well-justified, much deserved temper tantrum.

Of all the negative emotions—anxiety, guilt, depression, and anger—anger is somewhat unique. No one ever enjoys feeling anxious or guilty. A few people can enjoy feeling a little depressed, especially when they feel sorry for themselves. But lots of people can enjoy being angry— not all the time necessarily—but it can be quite satisfying now and then to blow up.

In fact, repeat this pattern for a while and it's possible to "get high" on anger, and eventually to get addicted to it. What better creature to give a parent their regular anger "fix" than some obnoxious adolescent, especially if the kid also is playing his own version of "Now I've Got You." So if you've totally had it, and want to become an accomplished "Now I've Got You" player, rather than just your average, crabby mother or father, here are some suggestions:

1. Think of the kid as a bad kid, even though he's really average or competent.
2. Always find something to criticize him for, no matter how small (a sign of success here is the teen always leaving the room when you enter).

3. Constantly evaluate and diagnose them; keep a sharp look out for any signs of something being wrong.

4. Voice all your worries to him and be consistent about it.

5. If you have an especially rotten day, get loaded at night, view the teen as the source of all your problems, then have a tantrum.

6. Constantly work on maintaining the exalted mental state of *Righteous Indignation.*

7. Also use and reuse The "Famous Lecture Series," including those old favorites:

"When I was a kid..."
"If it weren't for you..."
"When are you going to learn..."
"No one does anything around here but me..."
"If you'd just listened to me in the first place..."

There are other tactics that frustrated parents have found successful for ruining relationships with their children. If the kid's not around, you can go check their room for drugs, birth control devices, or just general messiness. You can also use clever arguments and interruptions to make their thinking look stupid, as well as listen in on phone conversations or try to find a diary to get more ammunition.

Blaming one's physical ailments on the adolescent has always been effective to induce guilt, and you are assured of an aggressive, angry response whenever you ask the little devil about his homework in the middle of his favorite TV show. Finally, a vital part of any consistent, warlike program should always involve grilling the child about simple requests, such as use of the car, where he's going, whom he'll be with, if he's dressed properly, and more. Be sure to repeat yourself, and respect the nine question minimum.

Seriously, if you feel you might be getting addicted to anger with your teenager, ask yourself three questions:

1. Am I getting quite angry at this child on a regular basis?
2. Am I going out of my way to look for things to get mad about?

3. Do I enjoy blowing up at this kid?

These things may be hard to admit, but try to be as honest as you can.

If you answer "Yes" to these questions, you are probably addicted to anger and you are either in—or about to be in—a state of war. That means that you will be deluding yourself that your efforts are geared toward helping the child shape up, while your real underlying motive will be to play "Now I've Got You."

What to Do

If you are in bad shape, or you are contributing constantly to a state of war, something needs to be done. How should you proceed? It depends on the issues, and there are no simple answers, but here are a few things to think about:

Individual counseling

Perhaps it would be a good idea to get yourself into counseling or psychotherapy. Lots of people have done it, and often with very good results. Research has proven over and over that depression, anxiety, and a whole host of other problems can be significantly altered through counseling with the right kind of professional. Sometimes certain kinds of medications can also be useful.

If you do find a counselor, make sure you like them. If you don't like the person or feel comfortable after two sessions, go find somebody else. Remember that you have a right to shop around.

Self-help

You say you don't need any help from a shrink and you'd rather go it alone? There are these days quite a few helpful books that have to do with handling psychological problems. Perhaps you can talk to a friend or professional to find one that might be good for you. There is a limit here, though. Give yourself two more months, and if you don't feel any better by then, find a professional therapist to talk to.

Marital counseling

Does your marriage need some work? Don't they all? Of course, no one's relationship with their spouse is perfect, but if this is one of the things that is bothering you a lot, it might be a good idea to give it some thought.

It's quite an easy thing to say you will go into marital counseling, but it's a totally different matter to actually do something about it. For starters, men don't usually like this kind of thing very much, and can be quite resistant to the idea. Men and women also commonly have quite different thoughts about what they expect out of a relationship. Women are normally much more interested in things like closeness, companionship, open communication, and orientation toward family. (It is probably mostly women who are reading this book in the first place.) Women, therefore, are usually the ones to initiate discussions about problems or some attempt at marital therapy.

Whether you are the husband or the wife in this situation, if you are thinking about marital counseling, here are some Do's and Don't's to remember:

- Try to pick your counselor together or, if one person is more reluctant to go along, let the reluctant one choose.
- Go in to see the counselor together the first time if you can.
- Before, as well as during any counseling, try to listen respectfully to the other person's point of view, even if you don't agree with it.

Research has shown that marital counseling can be quite helpful—if you can get into it.

Your work

Perhaps getting your act together means taking a long, hard look at your job situation. By this time many parents—mothers and fathers—may have been working on the same job for many years. Changing is certainly not easy, but take a look at several things about your job: do you spend a lot of time complaining to others about it? Do you consistently feel over-loaded and unappreciated? What do you think of your boss and how do you get along with him or her? How about coworkers? How do you feel on Sunday nights—or each morning when you wake up and realize it's a work day? On a scale from 1 to 10, how would you rate your job satisfaction?

Health

What kind of shape are you in? You may be tired of hearing this, but it is very helpful to get regular, strenuous physical exercise three to four times per week, especially if you are regularly feeling anxious, angry, or otherwise stressed. If you don't take your frustrations out on the racquet-ball court, you may very well take them out on your son or daughter. Do you have some physical problem that needs attention, or are you avoiding that physical exam because you are worried about possibly having something? It would be a good idea to check it out, rather than letting the worry fester in the back of your mind and make you more irritable.

Pass the Buck?

Finally, taking care of yourself may mean that you must temporarily pass the buck to your spouse when it comes to dealing with your troublesome teenager. This, of course, will make you feel guilty, but keep in mind that you will probably make things worse if you try to do something. You may also feel that your spouse will not do as good a job as you, or be as conscientious, in trying to handle problems. That's too bad, but unless it's an emergency, it's time for you to stay out of it. Some people say that's why God made two parents, so if one is out of commission, the other one can take over.

What if you don't have a spouse anymore, you simply have an "ex"? See if your ex can help out with the child, and if he or she can't, try to find a counselor for both you and your teen. If you do try to work out something with your ex, it may require laying to rest a lot of old hostilities.

If you do finally feel better and get your act together, what is the first thing you should do with your adolescent? Nothing! Go back and reevaluate your situation again to see if you still think there is major cause for concern.

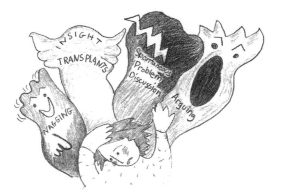

5

The Four Cardinal Sins

There are several things that are so destructive if used on a regular basis that we call them the "Four Cardinal Sins." These must be avoided if you are to have any chance at a decent relationship with your child or any chance at constructively solving problems. It is usually true that in families where there are significant difficulties with teenagers, these four mistakes are occurring all the time.

It's obvious, therefore, that there is something seductive or compelling about these tactics. Actually, they really don't deserve the label of "tactics," because they really are only primitive and impulsive emotional responses that occur without much thought. Any parent who reflects seriously on these things will have to admit that they don't do any good.

Before we describe the Four Cardinal Sins, we have something of a problem for parents who rated themselves as not doing too well. If you are really doing poorly and are under too much stress, you may very well be committing the Four Cardinal Sins more often than the average parent, because these four things are often used to blow off steam. At the same time you will be less able to control yourself and it will be hard for you to stop committing these minor atrocities.

So what are you going to do? Try to do your best to remember that if you are all stressed out, our rule is that you shouldn't be dealing with your teenager at all unless it's an emergency (a messy room or an earring on a male is not an emergency). The Four Cardinal Sins are all misguided attempts at dealing with problems, so if you're not supposed to be dealing with your kid at all, try to remind yourself to give up or let go—at least until you're doing better. This is extremely difficult, but do the best you can.

Here are the things that must be avoided at all costs:

1. Spontaneous Problem Discussions

This is a real killer. You see something that needs to be done, so you simply mention it to your kid, right?

Wrong! Here's a common scene:

"When are you going to start that chemistry paper?"
"What?"
"Your term paper for chemistry?"
"It's not for chemistry."
"Then what's it for?"
"It's for biology and I'll get to it."
"You've been saying that for two weeks."
"I said I'll get to it—get off my back!"
"If I didn't stay on you, you wouldn't do anything."
"If you don't shut up, you'll be doing the @#$% paper your-
    self!"
"Watch it, pal, I'm warning you."

Here the well-meaning parent sees a problem and, naturally, says something about it. What the parent is saying is perfectly valid and the parent is not trying to cause trouble.

The catch? The odds that the adolescent is also motivated to discuss this unpleasant subject at this time are about zero. In fact, spontaneous problem discussions almost always increase irritability and decrease cooperation. The child is almost always doing something else—even if it's only watching TV—and it takes a while to get "psyched" for talking about something unpleasant. You may feel this is stupid, but it's not. *It is a fact of human nature.* Chances are you feel the same way about people interrupting you with unpleasant things.

Sometimes spontaneous talks are unavoidable, of course, but otherwise what you need to do is make an appointment with your adolescent to discuss a problem. Tell him—short and sweet—what you want to talk about, and agree on a time to get together. Take him out to eat if you want.

> "I'm concerned about your grade in biology. When would be a good time for the two of us to talk this over? It won't take very long."

This is a better approach. Some parents' reaction to this, however, is something like, "Give me a break. What am I supposed to do, coddle the kid all his life!? Wouldn't want to interrupt the poor baby while he's watching television now, would we? After all, the poor thing just suffered through two hours of Nintendo while all his homework sat on the kitchen table."

Touchy, aren't we? This reaction is common and certainly understandable, but before talking to an adolescent about something sensitive, you'd better ask yourself if you are just trying to cause trouble or if you are really trying to solve a problem. If you know in your heart that the likely reaction to your request or statement is going to be negative nine times out of ten, you had better come up with a different approach.

2. Nagging

The second Cardinal Sin is closely related to the first, because it also usually comes up on the spur of the moment. Nagging can be defined as a set of repetitive, often hostile, verbal reminders about something that one person wants to see accomplished. It is usually directed at a second person who does not share the first person's enthusiasm for the project.

Nagging never works well, and—like the First Cardinal Sin—it usually just produces friction. But it is a very frequently used parental tactic when Mom or Dad is trying to get a child to do something. This brings up a very interesting paradox: why would a parent—being a basically reasonable, intelligent, and well-meaning person—use a strategy over and over that has been proven time and again not to work? There may be two answers. First of all, the parent may not know what else to do. Second, nagging is a spontaneous, poorly thought out action that comes primarily from emotional frustration.

Perhaps what is also behind nagging is a parental delusion that repetition will make the idea or request sink in. If asking the teen 22 times to clean his room didn't work, maybe the 23rd time will be the charm!

What is the antidote to nagging? First, be sure that what is going to be discussed is necessary, and then make an appointment. We repeat: don't open your mouth unless it's absolutely essential, then make arrangements to take the little darling out to dinner or something.

3. Insight Transplants

The third Cardinal Sin often takes the form of a parental lecture. The frustrated mother or father gets hold of their offspring and explains the facts of life to them about one thing or another. What the parent is really thinking—or hoping—goes something like this: "I will take this wonderful insight I have learned about life, put it into words, and send it through the air waves. It will enter my child's ears and proceed to his brain where it will take root, flower, and subsequently generate new and more productive behavior."

This type of thinking—if you really reflect on it—borders on psychotic delusion! Johnny is getting D's in his sophomore year of high school. Dad sits him down, explains that this type of behavior will not lead to a well paying job, and describes the study habits that made him valedictorian of his class twenty years earlier. Johnny responds by declaring, "Gosh, Dad, that sure makes a lot of sense," and he goes on to achieve all A's and B's during the remainder of his high school career.

That would certainly be nice, but it's not going to happen. Nevertheless, parents attempt Insight Transplants all the time. Once again, the point is not that what the parent is saying is stupid. On the contrary, it probably is very logical, but ironically, saying it either does no good or just causes irritation.

We often suggest to parents who are inclined to lecture their children that they open their eyes and closely examine the face of their child during the one-sided talk. Is there a scowl or a snicker there? Are the eyes rolling or is it the Great Stone Face routine? Many kids, instead of listening intently, are simply thinking, "Here's another repeat of item #43 from Father's Famous Lecture Series. How can I either shut him up or get out of here ASAP?"

This certainly doesn't mean that giving your children advice is dumb. But if you are doing it, 1) ask yourself how many times before you have said the same thing, 2) pay attention to the response you're getting, and 3) don't get your hopes up that immediate change is forthcoming.

4. Arguing

The final Cardinal Sin is arguing. Someone once said that the best advice he could give to parents of adolescents was never to argue with them. This may, in fact, be excellent advice. The three other Cardinal Sins discussed above often give birth to major arguments, which in turn damage relationships further and sometimes even lead to physical encounters or physical damage.

Surveys of parents asking what they find to be the most common and aggravating problems they run into with their adolescents invariably turn up arguing as a major difficulty. Mom and Dad often forget, however, that it always takes two people to have an argument. You cannot do it by yourself—so don't contribute to it.

Parents often ask, "What are we supposed to do if we don't argue, just keep our mouths shut and let them have their way?" Definitely not. When it is essential, you must try to see to it that your children are doing what they are supposed to, but it's very rare for anyone to be argued into submission. Arguing usually results in the battle lines being firmly drawn. Each person's ideas become more and more extreme, and sometimes they don't even mean what they say. The whole point of the "discussion" is to win and, if possible, find some clever way of making the other person look stupid.

Nothing is really gained from this. It just produces more conflict or— even if you can intimidate your child into submission—smoldering resentment that will cause more problems in the future. It's also likely that whatever you are saying you have said many times before, and you can guarantee that this will not be the time your message gets through.

What are your alternatives? Don't start a conversation that is bound to go nowhere; consider making an appointment if the matter is really important. Also, don't insist on having the last word. Let your son or daughter have the last word—provided it isn't horribly abusive, but then make sure they are doing what they should be (see the Major/Minor System in Chapter 11). If you do need to say something, simply say it directly and succinctly, and then shut up or leave; don't stick around to counter ridiculous arguments from your teen.

Spontaneous Problem Discussions, Nagging, Insight Transplants, and Arguing. If you surveyed teenagers, you'd probably find that these top their list of obnoxious parental behaviors. That fact by itself, however, does not mean you shouldn't talk. There are plenty of times when some kind of direction—stated once—is necessary.

The real issue here is that the Four Cardinal Sins don't solve anything and they do ruin relationships. And for some reason, they are *addictive*, even though they don't do any good. If they are not eliminated, it is likely that nothing else in this book will do much good.

The basic strategy for dealing with these four mistakes is the following:

1. If the problem you want to discuss is an MBA, shut up.
2. If it's important, make an appointment. Go out for dinner or a drive in the car.
3. If the discussion becomes an argument, don't argue. You say instead, "This conversation is stupid, I'm history" and leave.

6

Improving Your
Relationship

W hen you rated your relationship with your teen before, you were essentially describing the rapport the two of you have—how well you get along. Obviously, it is difficult to solve problems with someone if rapport is poor. In good relationships, on the other hand, conflicts will be easier to manage.

Before discussing more specific problem solving strategies, it will be helpful to look at some ways of trying to improve a relationship with an adolescent. These "tactics" require some effort, however, so there are a few things you should think about before plunging in. *First, are you sure you have the time, energy, and ability to bring these things off?* Remember that if you're in real bad shape yourself, you shouldn't even be reading this chapter yet.

Also you must decide, especially with chronic bad relationships, if it's too late. Sometimes it is, but don't give up too easily.

There are several ways of improving how you get along with a teen, and none of them is particularly easy. In addition to the absolute necessity of avoiding the Four Cardinal Sins, here are four other ideas:

1. Active Listening
2. Talking about Yourself
3. Shared Fun
4. Positive Reinforcement

In healthy relationships, these things probably happen more or less automatically and regularly. If your relationship with your child needs some work, however, and if you think you are ready, we'll describe the last four of these strategies.

Active Listening

Active listening is a way of listening and talking to someone sympathetically. It tries to accomplish two things: 1) to understand what another person is saying and thinking—from his or her point of view, and 2) to communicate back and check that understanding with the person doing the talking. The listener is an active participant in the conversation, rather than someone who just sits and nods from time to time.

Active listening is not easy, but it can be mastered. Once you get past the point of feeling artificial, "parrot like," or too passive, you can sometimes pleasantly knock the kids right off their feet with it. *Active listening should always be used at the beginning of any problem solving discussion.*

People who do counseling or psychotherapy have to use active listening when meeting a client for the first time. If they don't, they won't get the critical information they need to help solve problems. Picture this scene: a lady walks into a psychiatrist's office and says, "Doctor, I've been feeling rather depressed lately."

Before she has a chance to continue, the doctor says, "Depression? No big problem. I deal with that all the time and it's one of the most treatable things there is. Why, I'd venture to say that with some antidepressant medication and six to eight weeks of cognitive therapy you'll be feeling much better and after that we can take a look at..."

This is ridiculous, of course. This doctor is missing the boat in two ways. He is not getting all the information he needs, and he is also not doing anything to build a healthy and cooperative relationship.

The same thing is true in dealing with a child: if you don't listen, you may not get important information you might really need to know in order to realistically attack a problem. You also undermine the relationship further.

Imagine your 16 year old son went to a party on Friday night. On Saturday morning he gets up about 10:30 AM and comes down to the kitchen where you are reading the paper. No one else is home, and he says, "Well I finally did it. I got high last night for the first time."

How would you respond? Imagine, feeling rather startled and upset, you chose from the following:

> "I never want to hear that kind of talk again, young man!"
> "Well, fine, you're grounded until further notice."
> "Great, so now you're on drugs, huh? Listen, pal, when I
>   was a kid..."
> "How stupid can you be!? I told you those friends of yours
>   were nothing but..."

These, obviously, are not active listening responses (though they certainly are tempting). They also shut down the conversation, and the high-powered parent loses a shot at some very important information. What did the boy take? Marijuana, alcohol, PCP? What prompted this? Was it really the first time? Why is he telling me this now? (Actually, a teen's telling you something like this obviously implies either a pretty good relationship to start with, or an overwhelming desire on his part to provoke the daylights out of you).

Now let's imagine that you come up with this incredible, seemingly impossible response that goes something like this:

> *The Idiot*: "I got high last night for the first time."
> *You*: "Hold the phone, you caught me off guard. You want to
>   tell me what happened?"
> *The Jerk*: "You'll get all cranked out of shape."
> *You*: "Well, I can't guarantee I won't be upset or worried, but
>   I'll try not to scream."
> *The Moron:* "OK, maybe. Well, ah..., me and these new guys

went over to Lou's house, and they had some of this pot—
you know what that is?—he bought, and I'm like, 'Whoa,
what's this stuff,' and so John told me that it wasn't so bad,
so I...etc., etc..."

You're Like: "Sounds like you didn't want to look like a wimp
with these new guys, so you felt sort of pressured."

Your Son: "Yeah, although it wasn't so bad till I threw up. I
really couldn't say I was like really high, I was more like,
you know, not feeling too good or something..."

The Partially Relieved One: "You felt sort of embarrassed and
it wasn't so great?"

Mark: "I suppose."

You: "You sound a little disappointed."

This conversation is quite different and the teenager is opening up much more. The parent is also getting useful and important information (in this case it's more reassuring, though that certainly isn't always true). The parent is also exercising purposeful self-restraint by 1) not killing the conversation, 2) not killing the kid, and 3) knowing how to help the conversation along.

Adolescents can say many things that severely test one's patience, and very often a parent's spontaneous response is not very helpful. What would you say, for example, if your fifteen year old son said something like:

1) "I don't think sex before marriage is so bad."
2) "I think Camels taste a lot better than Winstons."
3) "I'm gonna get my ear pierced—all my friends have
   already."
4) "This family is really boring!"
5) "You know, I think your eating so much is going to kill
   you."

These kinds of statements can catch you off guard. If you are going to try to actively listen, remember that your goal is first to try to understand what the other person is thinking and saying, and second, to let them know that you are trying to understand. How do you do this? There are several different things that can be done, and once you get used to them the whole thing can feel quite natural.

Openers

You might start with what are called "openers"—brief comments or questions designed to elicit further information from your child. These can include statements such as:

1) "How's that?" (Sex)
2) "I'm listening." (Smoking)
3) "Let's talk about it—tell me what you're thinking."
   (Ear Piercing)
4) "Really?" (Joys of Family Living)
5) "Fill me in—so to speak—on what you're thinking."
   (Criticizing Your Eating Habits)

These comments require self-control, and are especially difficult when you are caught off guard. They may also appear incredibly passive or wimpy to you, but remember that active listening must precede any problem solving discussion. If discipline or other action is necessary, worry about it after you've gotten the facts.

Questions

An opener can be a question or it can be some other kind of statement, but usually further questions will be necessary. To be effective, *questions must not be loaded or judgmental*. Here are some bad questions:

1) "Why are you obsessed with sex at your age?"
2) "Why don't you stick with Camel straights and see if you can kill yourself?"
3) "Why in the h—l would you do a thing like that!?"
4) "So what's your problem today?"
5) "Why do you always hit me with the same old s—t!?"

These questions will inspire argument or silence. Here are some better questions that might keep the talk going as well as elicit more information (be prepared to be accused of sounding like a shrink):

1) "How many of your friends have had sexual relationships?"
2) "So you tried smoking and liked the taste?"
3) "How much does it cost to do something like that?"
4) "Why do you think we never do anything you like?"
5) "How come?"

In print alone, of course, we can't describe the *tone of voice* that should accompany these questions, but it should be readily apparent that any of the above could be totally ruined by a sarcastic, angry, belittling, condescending, or totally smart alec tone of voice.

Reflecting Feelings

If you are going to tell someone that you think you understand them, it's usually helpful to try to let them know that you can imagine how they must have felt under the circumstances they're describing to you. Again, you may be accused of sounding like a shrink, but if you are, just say, "Sorry, but I'm just trying to make sure I understand what you're talking about," or, "Give me a break, I'm doing my best to figure out what's going on!"

Imagine the five conversations above continued. At some point in the discussion, the parent might have an opportunity to say:

1) "You were really embarrassed thinking everyone else knew more about sex than you did."
2) "You're really curious about smoking."
3) "In your bunch of friends you're feeling left out without an earring."
4) "Sounds like you feel our family is almost depressing."
5) "You're afraid I won't live to see fifty."

Be careful here, because some adolescents don't like to admit or talk about their feelings to you, and even though you may be right on target, they may deny or take offense at what you're saying. As a kind of safeguard, the tone of all of the above statements can be changed some so they come across more as questions. Then it's more like, "Am I right that you felt this way?" The teen can then agree with you, deny, or reexplain the feeling. If you are still getting defensive responses every time feelings come up, scratch the feelings part, and stick to a more "intellectual" type of conversation, using just the other active listening tactics.

Checks or Summaries

From time to time during a talk, it is often helpful to check out with the other person whether or not you are "catching their drift," or really getting a good idea of what they're saying. These kinds of comments let you know whether or not you're understanding them correctly, but they also have a second purpose: they tell the adolescent that you're really listening to what they're saying.

Using our five examples again—but changing the order just a bit— the parent's conversation at some point might go like this:

2) "What you're saying is that if Dad and I can smoke—and we know it's not good for us—you should be able to as well?"
3) "Sounds like you think you'll fit in more, and also perhaps look better, if you can get your ear pierced?"
4) "You're telling me that you think we don't do much as a family, and when we do it's pretty boring to you?"
5) "You think I don't really care much about my health anymore, and the main reason is what my job has done to me?"
1) "So in your enlightened opinion, the old fashioned morality about sex is just so much hogwash, and now you and your peabrained friends can make your own rules while nobly striving to impregnate all the females in the western hemisphere!?"

Time out. Did we lose our cool in that last example? Yes. It's very difficult—especially when aggravated—to stay on track when trying to active listen. If you feel you're about to blow it, excuse yourself and come back later for another try.

This type of listening is also an *attitude*. Your attitude, not your child's. It's the attitude of sincerely trying to figure out what someone else is thinking even if you don't agree or even if it drives you nuts. Who knows, listen and you might learn something new.

Or you might have to lay down the law.

Talking about Yourself

With all this talk about active listening, it's all too easy to focus too much on your teenager. You can wind up constantly feeling like you're trying to "diagnose" the boy or girl to see if anything's going wrong. Teens quickly pick up this type of attitude and get defensive.

They may also start avoiding you.

One father described his son's behavior as "cave-itis," meaning that the boy spent almost all his time at home in his room. The cause for this, it turned out, was that the boy didn't feel it was safe to come out! Every time he showed up, he was "greeted" with statements like, "Is your homework done?", "Where did you get that shirt?", "I think it's about time for a haircut," and "Can you give me a little help around here today?"

A good antidote to this kind of relationship is to spontaneously talk about yourself. Horror of horrors. It's amazing how many parents seem to be almost phobic about discussing their own thoughts, concerns, or problems with their children. This is too bad, because many children of all ages would be very interested in hearing what their parents think about their jobs, their friends, about middle age, or about something interesting that happened to them that day.

Just so you don't get overly self-conscious, pay attention to two things before you plunge into self-revelation:

1. There can be no hidden message or moral in your story. Perhaps you were hoping that we had just come up with a sneaky way of getting some valuable point across. Sorry. That would only be a subtle version of one of the Four Cardinal Sins—the Insight Transplant routine. The point of your story can only be the inherent interest in the story itself.

2. The second rule, therefore, is pick something interesting. If you just relax and let yourself be spontaneous, it shouldn't be too hard to come up with something. It should be what you'd normally like to talk about anyway. How about:

"You won't believe what my boss said to me today!"
"I almost got into a fight in the Jewel parking lot this afternoon."
"I can't say I'm looking forward to my fortieth birthday."
"You know, when I was a kid, I used to love collecting baseball cards."

Some parents have trouble with this because they kind of feel they don't want to burden their children with their problems, or they feel as the parent they are only supposed to be interested in their children, or they have some kind of distorted idea that they don't want their children to know they might be unhappy about something. The old "Be Cheerful and Keep a Stiff Upper Lip" role model idea.

This is almost the equivalent of trying to present oneself as perfect, above it all, and able to handle anything. Can you see a problem with a parent coming across like this all the time, and combining it with a constant focus on the teen's problems? The "I'm just fine, but you still need a lot of work" idea is wonderful for creating belligerence in youngsters.

Other parents have trouble treating their kids as equals from time to time, even though sometimes this might be appropriate. Consider the possibility that *occasionally your kids might be able to active listen to you.* They might even have some good advice, now and then, for their parents.

Shared Fun

Find any two people who regularly have fun together and you will find a good relationship. But finding a common activity both you and your teen can enjoy can be harder than finding one for you and your spouse. However, doing something together that you *both* enjoy is—to a relationship—like water and fertilizer to a plant. It may sound corny, but it can work.

If you're having trouble finding something you can do with your son or daughter, at the end of the chapter we'll tell you what activity is usually the simplest and best bet.

When "trying" to have fun with your kid, several simple rules must be respected. Ignoring these precepts means certain death.

No problems!

When you're out horsing around, you are not allowed to discuss anything difficult or controversial. In other words, your long list of all the things you want your kid to change about himself or herself must be canned.

Imagine you and your fifteen year old son decided to go fishing. You are slowly floating down the river after having caught a couple of catfish, enjoying the sun and the calm rocking of the boat in the water. The fish remind you that you're hungry, so you mentally check your pockets for lunch money. There's enough—you're a good provider. Will your son be? Not if he keeps going like he did on that last science test. Better set him straight. So you comment, "I still can't believe you got a D on that biology exam." The fun is over.

One-on-one is better

Don't even try to take the whole family along if you're going out with your adolescent for some fun. For one thing, it's much easier to get along with someone when there are fewer people to complicate the situation. Also, parents of adolescents report *very* frequently that one of their biggest problems is sibling rivalry, and you won't have any fun if you are constantly having to keep two kids off each others' backs.

Many teenagers, in addition, have a nasty habit of not wanting to go out with the family because it isn't cool to be seen that way by your friends. (One thirteen year old girl always sat in the back seat, and then hit the floor whenever she thought she saw someone she knew.) Don't be offended, this is perfectly natural. It may be easier, though, for them to just go out with one parent.

Consistency

It certainly helps to be able to do something on a regular basis. That way the relationship is always getting some positive stimulation. It also usually means that things have to be planned in advance, which is good. If two people know that they are going to do something pleasant together on the weekend, it will tend to produce a "backup effect," meaning that this knowledge will help them get along better Monday through Friday.

No martyrdom allowed

Try to avoid doing something that the teen likes and that you hate. If you are not having a good time at a rock concert, for example, it is likely to show. The two of you may then argue or snipe at one another, and the whole experience becomes worse than doing nothing at all. Although it isn't easy sometimes, the two of you want to find something that you can both enjoy at the same time.

The sure thing (?)

Is there anything that an adolescent and their middle-aged parent can enjoy together? The closest thing to a sure thing here is probably going to a movie and then getting something to eat afterward. It's not that difficult to find a movie you can both enjoy, and if you're not getting along too well to begin with, this idea also has the advantage that you don't have to talk to each other much. Afterward, while you're eating, you can at least discuss the movie some.

What if your youngster refuses to do anything with you? Try not to act hurt or insulted. Remember that their overall job during adolescence is to get ready to leave home for good. Try to be as patient as you can, don't take it personally, and go back to using the other tactics for improving relationships.

So far, aren't these all wonderful ideas? A new relationship in no time! Seriously, are you positively certain that you have the energy and time to do any of this? Wishful thinking will not get you anywhere. OK then, on to the last tactic.

Positive Reinforcement

When you have a bad relationship with anyone, the idea of praising or commending them for something sounds like it's anywhere from impossible to insane. Yet this is one of the best ways to help improve how well you get along, providing you do it right.

Positive reinforcement simply means that you let the teenager know when you think they have done something well. You can do this while they're at it, or after they have done whatever it is. It might go something like this:

> "Looks like you put a lot of effort into that paper."
> "The grass looks real good."
> "Thanks for helping me move that stuff into the basement."
> "I can't believe how great your room looks!"
> "I think you handled that problem with your girlfriend better
>   than I would have in your shoes."

There's nothing too tricky about doing this, but again there are a few things you need to watch out for.

Tailor it

Some kids like effusive, elaborate praise and recognition, while others like a more brief, businesslike approach. Actually, by the time they are adolescents, more teens will be probably be in the second category, so it may be best to keep it short and sweet. Also, if you're not in the habit of doing this anyway—or if your relationship is pretty bad, you'd better start out small so you don't stand out like a sore thumb. But even if it feels a little awkward and embarrassing, just do it.

Keep it up

Consistency is important here too, but this can be very difficult, especially when the child regularly irritates you. Some parents have found it's helpful to work a sort of "mini-contract" with themselves, where they agree they will come up with three to five positive things per day to say.

Praise the behavior

You've probably heard the old advice about not criticizing the child, but criticizing the behavior? Interestingly, the same rule holds when it comes to positive feedback. It is better to point out what the kid did right and perhaps elaborate on that, rather than to try to say what a wonderful person the adolescent is. The latter approach comes across as inappropriate and embarrassing.

The 9 &1 rule

Don't leave your objectivity behind. Some parents say, "There's nothing good to say about them!" This is rarely true. There's a book that's been around for a while called *Catch Them Being Good*. The point is that if you are really paying attention and your attitude is right, you will see lots of things to reinforce.

Where Do You Start?

This was a long chapter, so let's summarize. If you decided earlier that your relationship with your teenager was not very good—or that you just would like to see it better before they leave home for good—you might want to give some thought to these rapport building strategies before it's too late.

The strategies in this chapter also vary in terms of how much *control* you have over them, and how much cooperation from the teen is required. Therefore, it makes sense to start with the ones over which you have total control. See if you can get something going there, then go on to some of the ones that require more help from the adolescent.

First, the Four Cardinal Sins absolutely must be avoided, otherwise you might as well not bother with the other tactics. But the Four Cardinal Sins are under your direct control. You don't need the teenager's help to stop doing them. The next tactic you control pretty much is positive reinforcement. Just do it in short bursts of enthusiasm. The kid doesn't have to respond. Next, don't just focus all your attention on your teen, however. Relax, let your hair down and talk about yourself some. Let the kids know you're human and imperfect and that there's more to you than. All they have to do is stick around briefly for your stories.

Then active listening can then be used to good effect, but it requires more input from the kids. It isn't so easy to learn and it takes practice, but it is extremely helpful and good for self-esteem.

If you've gotten this far, you're doing pretty well in improving the relationship. You might as well plunge into shared fun. It will be easier because you're talking better with much less threat of unpleasant surprises from problems popping up.

Part III

Four Parent Roles

7

Defining Your Job

Whoen something about your teenager is bothering you, it's a good idea to stop and think before doing anything. Shooting from the hip can cause a lot of trouble. You need to ask yourself two questions:

1. Does this problem need *my* attention or intervention?
2. If it does, how involved should I try to get?

Four Possible Roles

There are basically four roles a parent can consider using when responding to an adolescent's problem. They vary, of course, in their level of intrusiveness. From least intrusive to most involved they are:

1: Observer
2: Advisor
3: Negotiator
4: Director

As an observer you will stay out of it and merely watch what happens. This is an appropriate role for the MBA type of problem. You may get involved if the situation gets worse. As an advisor you will express your opinion to your child, but not more than once, and you must be ready for the possibility that they may not take your advice. If you choose to be a negotiator, you are going to sit down, talk the problem over, and come to some resolution. Finally, if you take on the role of director, you are going to impose a solution when you feel a problem is serious and your adolescent is not handling it well.

How do you decide which place to start? The evaluation of your situation you did in Chapter 2 will help. Several things should be kept in mind.

1. How is your child doing in general?

In general, the better your child is doing, the less you need to be involved, and the more you can stay with observer or advisor roles. As the kids get older, they also should also become more independent and competent, so you will treat an seventeen year old much differently on some issues than a thirteen year old. Kids who are having a lot of trouble, however, will need more involvement, but this does not mean large and regular doses of the Four Cardinal Sins!

2. How good is your relationship?

If you get along well with your teen, any kind of intervention is easier. They will accept advice from you more easily, and it is also easier to talk things over when negotiation is necessary. You won't need to take charge as much. A bad relationship, however, may mean you have to be a director more often, and negotiating and advice giving become almost ridiculous or impossible. If your rapport with the teen is really bad, make sure you don't open your mouth unless you have a very good reason.

3. Your state of mind

Make sure you're in good enough shape to try to handle a problem, otherwise you're likely to do more harm than good with your emotional dumping. If you're under too much stress, it's almost inevitable that you will attempt to use tactics that are too intrusive. Your kids will resent your unnecessarily sticking your nose in their business, and you'll be off to the races.

4. How serious is the problem?

With less serious difficulties, you should be sticking more with the less intrusive alternatives. Keep in mind that your level of aggravation about a problem is not always the measure of the real seriousness of the problem. Examples? Earrings on males, jeans with holes, messy rooms, sibling rivalry, eating junk food and other MBAs.

In trying to decide what role to play, therefore, your general philosophy should be to stay out of their problems unless it is necessary for you to get involved. The kids are at the point in their lives where they are supposed to be handling things more and more on their own, and inappropriate attempts at direction from you can cause useless irritation and conflict.

Some people refer to this issue as "problem ownership." Whose problem is it, really, and do you absolutely have to make it yours? If you have a teen who's generally doing well academically, for example, but who is currently getting an F in Spanish because he hates the teacher for some weird reason, perhaps you can legitimately stay out of it. Or you have an average child who is dragging his feet in looking for a job, or wearing some kind of weird T shirt to school, maybe your "help" isn't needed and you can let the big, bad world instruct your youngster.

Getting Mixed Up

A lot of trouble occurs when a parent decides to take one role and their child assumes that another role would be more appropriate. Sixteen year old Michelle, for example, is going on a double date Saturday night. She and a girlfriend and two guys will go to Chicago on the train to see a concert in the evening. The four kids will return together afterwards on a train that departs at 11:30 PM. In the middle of the week, however, the plans change. Neither of the guys can go. Michelle informs her parents that she and her girlfriend will go alone. Dad says no way and a royal argument ensues.

Part of the problem here is the role each person thinks Dad should take. Michelle thinks Dad should be only an observer—or at most an advisor. Dad thinks he should be a director:

Teen's Choice   vs   Parent's Choice

√

Observer
Advisor
Negotiator
Director   √

A lot of arguments take place when this unspoken difference of opinion occurs. The "discussions" are very confusing because two things (the actual problem *and* the role) are being talked about at the same time.

What to do? If you're the parent, *try to make up your mind what role is correct in the first place and then stick with it.* Tell your teen what role you are going to take. If you have chosen a less intrusive role, such as advisor or observer, stay with it even if you get anxious or angry.

Your son, for example, is a junior in high school. He has just purchased a CD that consists of some of the most repulsive rap "music" you have ever heard. You decide, however, to shut your mouth and merely be an observer. (Actually, you don't even want to listen to the stuff.) One night, though, you and he start discussing his musical preferences. You express your opinion that his CD choices bear no remote resemblance to music and are also obscene. He says your music is sappy and has no real social message. One thing leads to another and you tell him he cannot play his junk in your house anymore.

Mistake. Anger has pushed you from observer to an inappropriate director role.

By the way, who was right in our other example, Michelle or Dad? The answer is Dad. His choosing the director role there was what he should have done. Two sixteen year old girls are not going downtown to the big city and back by themselves on a Saturday night.

8

Observer

As an observer, you are basically doing nothing. You are trusting your child to handle things and you will stay out of it. Your daughter, for example, has a new friend that you don't particularly care for, but she's generally doing well and you respect her opinion. Or your son is getting to bed somewhat later than he used to. You're worried that it may affect him during the day, but so far he seems OK. You can keep a watchful eye on what's happening, or—if worse comes to worse and you still think you should keep your mouth shut—you can simply grin and bear it.

Watching and Listening

Just observe how the child is handling a problem and maybe do some sympathetic listening. This is often an excellent idea for competent or average kids and nonessential problems, such as a messy room, a diet, a friend you don't like, or even a temporary drop in a grade.

Remember the "letting go" notion and let the teen handle it. Don't give unwanted advice that only irritates, but if you can, do some active listening. Maybe you'll learn something reassuring. Then again, maybe you won't. But if you do come upon some more disturbing information, take some time to think about it before doing something more assertive. Remember that anger and anxiety can push parents into roles that are not right for the situation.

Grin and Bear It

Before intervening, try more aggressively to "let go" by using the "Grin and Bear It" approach. Actually, you really don't need to grin. Unfortunately, however, there are many times when an adolescent can be doing something that irritates the daylights out of you, but you still should not get too involved in it. Maybe they're eating junk food after school and you think they should have fruit. Perhaps you don't like the way they talk to one of their friends, or they always study with the radio on.

How can you avoid saying something about these major violations of human nature? It's certainly not easy when you're really angry, but try to first remind yourself that with kids who are generally doing well—or even average kids, you want to encourage independence. They have to leave home soon and you can't go with them. Second, if you have a problem child and are upset about some nonessential problems, you don't need anymore hassles than you already have, so try to bite your tongue. Is another argument about the same garbage going to really help? Third, if your relationship with the teen isn't too good and the problem isn't too horrible, wait on the problem for awhile and try to aggressively work on improving your relationship. Then you may have a little more leverage when it comes time to try to intervene or help.

The Awful Scale

Many parents have gotten a lot of benefit from what is sometimes called the "Awful Scale." What you do here is create a kind of subjective/ objective scale that ranges from 0 to 100, and you use it to rate the "awfulness" of the different things that might happen to you in your life. Something rated 0 would not bother you at all. A rating of 5 would be a minor hassle, while a rating of 90 would be a pretty horrible occurrence. An event qualifying for a score of 100 would be something that would make you permanently miserable.

Once you have the general idea of the Awful Scale, you have to practice rating different things. So what would you rate a flat tire on your car at the end of a long work day? Some people say 10, some 20 or 30. What if you broke your right arm, and you are right handed? 30 or 40? What if your house burned down? Most parents say 60 or 70. What if your spouse died? Some people say, "It depends on the day," but most people put this in the 90 to 95 category.

Do you know what almost all parents consider to be the worst thing that could happen to them? The death of a child. People will say "That would be 110," or "I can't even imagine it." But most parents agree that it would be as close to 100 as anything can get.

With this perspective in mind we return to some of the actual problems that parents are concerned with in their children. Your male son comes home sporting a new, dangling earring and carrying a progress report with two F's on it. What would you rate that? Many parents say something like, "Why that little creep! That gets an 85 or 90 easy!"

We then try gently and respectfully to point out that the rating for the earring and the grades is only 10 points away from the rating for the death of the child! This obviously can't make any sense (even though some parents say, "If he keeps this up I'll murder him myself!"). What is seriously needed is another long look at how bad the problem really is, and what usually happens is that—upon further review—the original rating will not stand as it was. Realistically, the true "awfulness" is most often quite a bit less than what was first thought or felt.

So Mom and Dad are asked to "re-rate" whatever it is that is bothering them. This certainly doesn't mean that everything becomes a 0, but it does mean that, on the scale from 0 to 100, an earring probably merits a rating of 0.0067 and the grades perhaps 4.23.

What kinds of problems and in what kinds of situations might you consider only observing? For any kids you should stay away from the MBAs. For competent kids, you might stay out of concerns such as bedtime, dating, work, use of money, and selection of friends.

What if you feel you *are* being objective about the problem, but you still can't stand it or think you really should do something? The next least intrusive role is that of Advisor.

Advisor

A n advisor is a person who is hired to consult with someone, but there is a condition. The condition is that the person who receives the advice has the right to accept or reject it. This is the role we are talking about here.

"I wish you'd cut your hair shorter," "Please clean your room this weekend," "If you want my opinion, I think you're trying to push your boyfriend around too much," and "I think it would be a good idea if you got your homework done before we leave," are all potentially legitimate consultant statements. They are attempts to give advice, and with average to above kids and fairly good relationships, they stand some chance of getting a positive response. As an advisor, however, you are still only a consultant to the child, which means *you are not using power and the adolescent has the right to reject your advice.*

If your advice or request doesn't change the situation, you have two alternatives (neither alternative is to repeat your "advice" over and over). With small problems, you may just go back being an observer and the "Grin and Bear It" approach. But if you feel the issue is more important, you may want to go on to the next parent role which involves negotiating.

If you are going to consider trying to be an advisor to your child, don't shoot from the hip. There are a few considerations you should think over before you open your mouth.

You probably weren't hired for the job

If you are going to give your son or daughter some friendly counsel, remember that it is your idea to do this and not theirs. If they ask for your opinion, fine, but if they don't, be careful. For example:

> "Better comb your hair before you leave."
> "What?"
> "You heard me—you can't go to school looking like that."
> "Who asked you, anyway?"
> "Watch that tone of voice, young lady."
> "For your information, this is how they wear it nowadays!"
> "This may be the new age, but you look like a witch, and I'm
>   not letting you out of the house like that!"
> "Dad, it's my hair—not yours!"

The teen has a point—this is MBA territory. She's also getting mad about the unsolicited consultation—from a male of the species.

Giving advice vs taking charge

As we mentioned before, before you say anything, make up your mind what role you're in. Some of the biggest conflicts between teenagers and their parents occur because the parent feels one role is appropriate (e.g., director), and the child feels another role is correct (e.g., observer or advisor).

If advising only is appropriate, try to stick with it, even if you get angry. The conversation above, for example, might continue in two different ways. In the first scenario, Dad forgets, because he gets mad, that he shouldn't be telling his 17 year old daughter what her hair style should be:

> "It may be your hair, young lady, but I'm your father!"
> "And an internationally known hair stylist, no doubt!"

"That's it, smart alec! Upstairs! Comb! Read my lips, or
   you're not setting foot out of this d—m house!"

Bad ending. Dad's anger at his daughter is pushing him into an
inappropriate director role. Now let's imagine instead that the conversation goes something like this:

"Listen, your hair really looks sloppy."
"Dad, what do you know about hair styles for teenage girls?"
"Enough to know it's your funeral."
"I like it like this."
"Fine, be my guest."

Here Dad is not happy, but he is not getting into something he should
stay out of. Kids do have some weird hair styles. Have you ever seen an
adolescent girl who used to be cute, but who now has orange hair and a
partial crewcut? Remember we're from different planets.

If directing is appropriate, on the other hand, stick with it and don't
be intimidated by the child's anger. In this example Dad tries a little
friendly advice first:

"I'm leaving—see you later."
"Don't be too late, honey. What time you coming home?"
"Two or three."
"Not! Curfew's twelve."
"Dad, my friends will laugh at me. I *am* 16!"
"And I'm 42. Be back at twelve."
"Oh, for pete's sake!" (Exit Miss Grump)

Here Dad is taking charge, and he should. Hours for a 16 year old are
not subject to the whim of the child.

Spontaneity can be dangerous

Unwanted advice is a problem by itself, but when the unasked for wisdom
comes out of the blue, things are doubly rough. The response is very likely
to be irritation and absolutely no receptiveness to whatever you are trying
to say.

Can you get around this? You can try, and here are several ways. First, see if you can get "hired" as a consultant to your teen, or at least warn them that some discussion may be coming. You might say something like, "You mind if sometime we talk some about these kids you've been with the last couple of weeks?"

Second, if you think consulting is the appropriate role for you with this kid and this problem, clarify out loud before any discussion that you only want to talk, that you may or may not give any advice, and finally that any advice you give can be used or not as your youngster sees fit. Make up your mind first that this is what you want to do. This will help you not feel like a wimp as a parent (you're supposed to let go more and more), and it may also help you *not* jump into a heavier role you don't belong in if the teenager makes you angry. It will also help your child be less defensive, knowing that the final decision will be up to them.

Third, in any discussion about a problem, you must active listen first. Unfortunately, it may be true that few teens are going to want to listen to your opinions much in the first place. You increase your chances of being listened to, however, by having the patience to hear them out before you speak.

Do something weird!

Your adolescents aren't the only ones who can do strange things. You can, too! If you are about to give out some potentially unpopular piece of advice, do it in some unusual way.

One of the tactics that many parents have found very helpful here is to go out somewhere special to talk things over. You can actually take them out to dinner. This accomplishes several things. It is fun, or at least it can be. It also says to the adolescent that you are serious enough to do something really awesome! Rather than trying to communicate your concern by yelling or nagging, you underline it in a pleasant—but perhaps equally graphic—manner.

Another thing is to write out your thoughts and give it to them. Parents often forget that the sound of their voice can be very irritating, especially when they are worried. And parents often also forget a very basic principle: no one likes to be interrupted, and at home the most common cause of interruptions is the result of someone else's voice. The voice seems to be either telling you something or asking you to do something. When the kids were little and they would say "Mom," for example, there were different tones and inflections to the way "Mom" was said. One meant I want something, another meant I hurt myself, another meant my brother is teasing me again.

Your voice has the same ability to reflect different possible meanings. Many of them are not pleasant to your kids, and usually children can immediately tell the "anger tone" from the "request-time tone" from the "excited-pleasant tone." There is also a style and a tone that accompanies advice, and if you find this is continually irritating your teen, you are probably being a nag and you should consider writing rather than talking. A brief note is sometimes more helpful. Some parents have even drawn simple cartoons to try to get their point across. Now that's weird!

Advice is cheap and rarely followed

Be realistic and accept the fact that, even though your ideas may be perfectly valid—and parents rarely give stupid advice—it is not likely to be acted upon. You are in the odd—but very common—position of having something quite reasonable to say, but saying it either does no good or it aggravates the relationship.

It's obvious, therefore, that being an advisor may not work (at least as far as you're concerned). Many frustrated parents, however, when advice fails, take their pleasant request and repeat it 400 times, tack on one of the Famous Lecture Series, or beg, plead, threaten, nag, or yell. These are just different versions of the Four Cardinal Sins; you'll blow off some steam, but you won't do any good.

If advice and simple requests don't work *and you feel the issue is still important (not an MBA)*, you can try negotiating and then, if necessary, get even heavier handed.

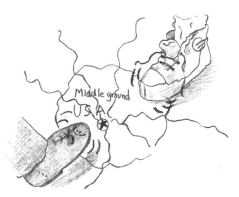

10

Negotiator

The beginning of an attempt at negotiation might go something like this: "We've got a problem here and sometime I'd like to talk it over with you." What you are doing here is recognizing that the child is older now, and that they should have some say about many of the things that they do. Negotiating is also a statement that you feel it is important that you be involved, because you think the problem is serious, or perhaps because it affects other family members in addition to just the one adolescent. But you are saying that—up to a point—you are willing to bargain or make a deal.

Although negotiating doesn't have to be anything horribly fancy, it is critical that certain minimal guidelines be followed:

1. Agree to negotiate

You can't just plunge in. Remember the rule outlawing attempts at spontaneous problem solving discussions, and never insist on an immediate talk unless it's a total emergency. Also, don't bring up the idea of having a talk when you are already pretty cranked out of shape about something; chances are your teenager will just go nuclear on you, you won't get anywhere, and it will be just that much harder to bring it up again.

How do you broach the subject of making a deal with the kids? Imagine these possibilities:

"When's a good time for you to talk with me about your room?"

"You may not be too thrilled by this suggestion, but sometime in the next couple of days I want to sit down with you and talk about college."

"I can't say I care for your new work schedule too much. Can we go over it together sometime?"

"We gotta talk about your smoking. Not now, but tell me when's good."

In responding to these opening comments, kids may actually attempt to talk about the problem prematurely. When they are caught off guard like this, however, it is unlikely that you are going to have a profitable pow-wow. It is more likely that—in the interests of serving their budding independence—they are going to try to just get you off their backs as quickly as possible. There are two ways they can do this. The first is to try to minimize your worries and make light of the problem:

"What's the big deal?"

"Oh, Mom."

"Just chill out, will ya, I'll take care of it."

You, however, have already thought it over and decided the problem is important, or you wouldn't have brought it up, right? So you respond to these comments by telling them that you don't want to discuss it right away, but that you feel it's important and you do need to go over it. When is a good time for them? Don't get suckered into talking about the problem with an uncooperative adolescent.

The second way the teen may try to get rid of you is to attempt to provoke a fight:

"Why don't you mind your own business?!"

"You smoked when you were a kid."

"Why are you always harping at me?"

Don't get sidetracked and stumble stupidly into one or more of the
Four Cardinal Sins. You are being baited. Keep in mind what your major
goal is here (it's not murder). *Your objective is only to make an appointment with the youngster to talk.* If they refuse to talk, and you still feel the
problem is important, you will be going on to the director role.

2. Pick a good place and time to talk

Go to a quiet room or take them out somewhere or go to dinner. Sometimes
a long ride in the car is helpful (you don't have to look right at each other).
It's great if you can plan something enjoyable to do *after* the discussion,
but this doesn't always work. Make sure there won't be a lot of interruptions from other family members and definitely no possibility of phone
calls.

3. Define the problem

Assuming that you've survived the process so far, your next goal is to
define the problem (then you will try to bargain, if necessary). Here you
have something of a difficulty, though. You want to listen to them to begin
with, but you're the one who brought up whatever it was in the first place.

The best answer to this dilemma is probably for you to say what the
problem is *very briefly*, then ask them for their thoughts. Don't go rattling
on and getting all excited. Why, if you keep trying to talk to your kids like
that you'll never get anywhere with anything! How many times have we
already said that you can't do that! I don't know what it's going to take for
you as a parent to get it through your head that this kind of thing...

Sorry. Where were we? The teen is talking first and you are using
active listening. Give him 5-10 minutes, longer usually isn't necessary.
Don't interrupt, roll your eyes, or make faces like they're an idiot. Just
listening and not arguing does not have to imply that you agree with
everything the adolescent is saying.

You may not like what you hear. Try to keep your cool, but if you find
yourself really upset after the teen has talked, say something like, "Listen,

a lot of this is new to me and I need some time to think it over. Give me a day to get used to all this, and then maybe we can sit down and we'll finish it."

If you're not too upset, ask the child to not interrupt you while you take 5-10 minutes to explain your side of things. Stay calm and try not to accuse or blame. Remember, if the issue is something like a messy room, loud music, or appearance, the adolescent may not feel the issue is much of a problem.

4. Let's make a deal

Assuming you've gotten through the earlier negotiation phases alive and with the problem clarified, you must now come up with a solution. (Actually, some of the time you may not need a solution, because you learned that the thing was not as big a deal as you thought, but usually you won't be this lucky.)

To bargain or make a deal, don't get too pushy about your own ideas—even if you feel they're just brilliant. Try to get the teen to make suggestions first and give them careful consideration. You might start the solution part of the conversation by saying something like:

> "Well, it's obvious we don't agree, but that doesn't mean we can't come up with some compromise. What do you think?"
> "Tell me what you think would be fair to you and everybody else."
> "What kind of arrangement do you think would work here?"

The sign of a good bargain is that there is something in it for everyone, but also that everyone has to give up a little something, too. The best solution is *one that the teen comes up with* that also helps you feel better. If you can't agree with your child's initial proposal, support the good parts of their idea and suggest some modifications.

Here are some examples of possible bargains:

1. Loud music. Dad agrees to buy Mark headphones for the stereo if Mark will promise to wear them—and not use his large speakers—whenever anyone else is home.

2. Phone. Melissa can talk on the phone as much as she wants as long as her grades don't drop below a C average and as long as she pays the extra on phone bills over $50/month.

3. Smoking. Mom and Dad agree to stop nagging 18 year old Tom about his smoking, as long as he no longer smokes in the house.

4. Hair. Parents will pay for Jim's haircut as long as the mop is not left more than two inches below his collar.

What if the teen doesn't want to suggest anything out of belligerence or because he feels it's not a problem? You have a choice: either go back to the observer role (forget giving more advice and shut up), or move on to the taking charge roles (next chapter).

If you are able to come up with a solution, it's often helpful to write it down. Some people even sign it like a contract, though the kids often feel this is stupid. Try to write it out anyway; it helps you remember what you said and it makes the agreement feel more solid.

If your agreement works well, a little brief, friendly positive reinforcement would be in order. If it doesn't work, don't have a fit. Go back to the drawing boards, hang on to the good parts of your deal, and see if you can agree on the necessary changes. Follow the same basic negotiation format described above.

With good relationships, negotiating is obviously easier than with lousy ones. On the other hand, try to keep in mind that if the relationship is not very good in the first place (and the problems are not emergencies), you should spend perhaps a month or more working on how you get along before tackling any issues.

Also, since problem kids present multiple problems, *be sure to stick with one problem at a time*. Although a lot of things may irritate you, you certainly can't solve them all at once, and mentioning more than one at a time is likely to just amount to mudslinging.

Just as with the previous roles, negotiating doesn't always work. There's so much that can go wrong. Kids can refuse to talk with you. Attempts at talking can turn into screaming matches. Agreements can be made, but not followed up on.

What do you do if negotiating fails? Try it again! Or, you may conclude that, after all, this problem is really not worth all this trouble, so you Grin and Bear It. Don't forget to use the Awful Scale to help you settle down.

If you decide that the problem still is important, take a deep breath and go on to the next chapter.

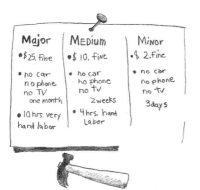

Major	Medium	Minor
• $25. fine	• $10. fine	• $2. fine
• no car no phone no TV one month	• no car no phone no tv 2 weeks	• no car no phone no tv 3 days
• 10 hrs. very hard labor	• 4 hrs. hard Labor	

11

Director I: The Major/Minor System

For too many families there are times when no amount of talking or consulting is going to do any good. Things have gone too far, problems have gotten too serious, and relationships have been too bad for too long. When things get to this point, it is time for Mom and/or Dad to draw the line.

This obviously isn't easy to do, and for many parents the idea of trying to tell their adolescents what to do—or to try to force them to do it—brings up images of ferocious retaliation. The bad news is that teens can certainly manipulate and fight back. The good news is there are only six ways they can do it, and if the couple—or single parent—is ready, this can be managed.

If you feel it is time to take charge regarding something in the life of your teenage youngster, you have two choices. Both require clear thinking, emotional self-control, and hard work:

1. The Major/Minor System
2. Evaluation and Counseling

The Major/Minor System

When a problem is serious enough (drugs) or interferes directly with your life (loud music), you have a definite right to take charge and become the director of a solution. If the child is uncooperative, the relationship is poor, and all other steps haven't worked, the use of power is legitimate—provided that this use is not just a camouflaged attempt at waging war .

First, if both parents are living at home, sit down together, define the problem, and decide exactly how the two of you are going to take a stand on a particular issue. Also, look at the chapter on Testing and Manipulation, predict what types you'll be likely to get and prepare to handle them.

How do you take a stand? You give a written warning first, then you use the Major/Minor System.

The warning is a message to your teen that certain behavior is unacceptable, and if it doesn't change within a certain time, you will institute consequences. Your warning is often better written than spoken, because the child has learned to either dismiss your words or argue with you consistently, so there is no way of having a productive conversation. So remain silent and don't attempt the impossible: talking. It's "Actions are louder than words" time.

Here is an example of a warning note to a 16 year old girl. The situation is that she is an average kind of kid and her relationship with her parents is OK:

Dear Mary,

Smoking in your bedroom is something we can no longer tolerate. Talking about it with you has been useless.

If you stop smoking in the house from now on, we will take you and a friend out for pizza on Dec. 5, or we can help you arrange some other outing of your choice. If you do not stop, as of Dec. 5, your phone privileges at home will be removed until you do stop.

Love,
Mom and Dad

No more talking or nagging. It is critical that you shut up at this point. Your next step will be *doing something*, not words.

If the child responds positively, there is nothing wrong with rewarding them with a dinner, increase in allowance, special use of the car, trip, tape, outing with a friend, party, or whatever. It's a friendly sign and helps prevent war. The size of the reward may be proportional to the size of the problem.

What if they don't respond? Now it's action using the Major/Minor System. This means that to begin with, you classify the problems you have as "big deals" or "little deals." Actually, you could have three or four classifications if you wanted. You might consider something like staying out overnight a Major, leaving your tools out a Minor, and cutting a class at school a Medium offense (3 cuts or more is a Major).

You then decide what consequences will follow for Major offenses, Minor offenses, and in between. When the misbehavior occurs, you then institute the consequence without yelling, lecturing, or playing "Now I've Got You!"

> *A guaranteed law of adolescent psychology is this: repeatedly engaging in one or more of the Four Cardinal Sins will always obliterate the effectiveness of any consequence or punishment.*

Parents often wonder, though, just what kind of power or influence they still have when it comes to their teens. It's true that it's harder to come up with power over teens; little kids you can drag to their rooms. However, you still may have two kinds of power: "relationship power" and "amenity control" power.

Relationship power is based partly on the fact that long ago you were a powerful person in the child's eyes who could do anything and who totally controlled the child's fate. It is also based on whatever pleasant experiences or "bonding" you two have shared over the years. In good relationships, this respect and love are still active. They are somewhat weaker in average relationships, but still not totally gone even in bad ones. This relationship power is your primary asset in trying to be an advisor or negotiator, but if you regularly engage in arguing, nagging, lectures, and yelling, you throw whatever leverage you have here out the window.

Amenity control power is based on the fact that you still control to varying degrees many of the conveniences your child enjoys in this world, and—believe it or not—you have the power to withdraw them. Like what, you say? Like money: allowances and loans; cars: chauffeuring (13-15 year olds) and use (16-18); food, laundry service, phone, TV's and sometimes radios, and often more (like electricity and toothpaste!). You also provide these without even thinking. You may never have thought of making a deal with the adolescent like, "I'll provide these services as long as you behave yourself." But you can.

You also had better be talking about serious problems and not MBAs.

In addition to temporary removal of selected amenities, things like grounding or chores are also used with the Major/Minor System. However, looking at the list of possible consequences, you can see that some require more cooperative kids in order to be used. With problem kids and bad relationships, it's better to use things that you have more control over, such as fines (from allowance), car use or rides, phone (it can be locked), or TV's (they can even be removed).

Here's a brief summary of Major/Minor System:

1) All previous steps have failed.
2) The problem is important.
3) If both parents are living at home, sit down with spouse,
   define the problem precisely, decide how to take a stand,
   and prepare for testing.
4) Give written warning.
5) Reinforce compliance.
6) If no compliance, implement consequences.
7) Stick to it with no arguing.

A three category (Major/Medium/Minor) system might look something like this:

<u>Major</u>: offenses could include: out all night, physical violence, drinking and driving, party without permission at home with no parents. Consequences for Major offenses could include: $25 fine, no TV one month, no phone or car one month, 10 hour chore or project, or grounding for two weeks (can't leave house except for work or school).

Medium: offenses might be behavioral trouble at school, smoking (13-15 year olds), friends at home without permission. Consequences for Medium offenses could include: $10 fine, no TV two weeks, no phone two weeks, 4 hour chore, or one week grounding.

Minor: offenses might include leaving your tools out, leaving house unlocked, forgetting to feed dog in morning. Consequences might be: $1-2 fine, no TV 3 days, no phone 3 days, or 4 day grounding.

One of the easiest applications of the Major/Minor System involves the problem of chores. We use what we call the "Docking System." The Docking System works best when the child has an allowance (next best is if they have a source of money from a job). Suppose there is a problem with things like not feeding the dog, dirty dishes left around the house, not getting laundry down to the washer, or not taking out the garbage, even though these jobs have been clearly defined. The Four Cardinal Sins have not worked (surprise!), nor has advice or negotiating.

The frustrated parent informs the adolescent that they have good news and bad news for them. The good news is that if the garbage is not taken out, for example, the parent will do it for the teen! The bad news is that the parent charges for this service, and each time they have to do it, it will cost so much in cash or off the allowance. That's it.

If the Four Cardinal Sins are avoided, one of two things will happen. The kids will shape up and begin to do their chores better, or the parent will do the work and get paid on a regular basis. At least then Mom or Dad doesn't have to feel things are so unfair.

Negotiating the Major/Minor System

With some situations, where the child and the relationship aren't so bad, negotiating and directing can be sort of combined. Assume you have already set up the System and an offense has occurred. Often it works well to let the teen pick the consequence from the list. If he refuses to pick or delays, you pick and impose. The child may even negotiate the system with you to begin with, after talking by itself has not worked.

When setting up the system—and especially when imposing consequences—be prepared for certain predictable statements from your kids:

1. "This is stupid."
2. "I don't care what you do to me."
3. "My friends think you guys are weird."

Don't pay much attention, and don't smirk or act superior. Ninety per cent of the adolescents who say "I don't care" do care. Just be quiet, do what you have to, and be prepared for more testing and manipulation.

If the Major/Minor System doesn't work, testing is extreme and prolonged, or the whole thing is just too much of a hassle, it may be time for a professional evaluation and perhaps counseling.

12

Director II:
Evaluation and Counseling

T here's no rule that says you must be able to handle all problems
yourself. Considering professional advice might not only be a very
good idea, it may be essential. There are, as a matter of fact, certain
problems that you should never attempt to handle on your own. Some of
the more common ones that adolescents experience—as well as their signs
and symptoms—are described below.

Anxiety Disorders

In some ways it may seem that anxiety and adolescence are synonymous,
but many unfortunate adolescents experience extremely large doses of
anxiety that make their lives miserable. Anxiety disorders are characterized by an excessive fear of something, and that something varies
depending on the type of disorder. Anxiety disorders also devastate self-
esteem—as anxiety level goes up, self-esteem goes down. Unlike children, teenagers who experience these problems know that their anxiety is
excessive, but this simply adds to their feeling of embarrassment and
stupidity. It's not surprising, therefore, that these teens usually don't like
to talk about their problem.

Anxiety disorders tend to run in families, they are usually more common in girls, and often they start during early adolescence. Recent studies indicate that they may be much more common than we have realized in the past. To be diagnosed they must been going on for some time, usually more than six months.

In *generalized anxiety disorder* the teenager worries about a number of different kinds of things, from performance at school to the possibility of nuclear war to being on time. The child cannot control the worries, and they may impair concentration and cause excessive fatigue, restlessness, irritability and difficulty sleeping. The prevalence rate for generalized anxiety disorder is approximately 3%.

With *social anxiety disorder* (or social phobia) the core fear is fear of embarrassment in social situations. The adolescent has an excessive worry—that can border on panic—of looking stupid in situations such as public speaking. The teen may also avoid things like eating in public, for fear others will see their hands shake, or talking to new people, for fear their voice will sound shaky. When these situations are unavoidable, the physical distress accompanying them is considerable, and can involve blushing, sweating, tremors, and diarrhea. The estimated prevalence of this disorder ranges from 3% to 13%, and it is unclear if it is more common in boys or in girls.

About 4% of children and younger adolescents experience *separation anxiety disorder*. This is characterized by an unusually strong fear of leaving home or of being separated from one's family or caretakers. Teens who have this problem often worry about their parents being killed. They may have trouble going to school in the morning or going to sleep by themselves at night.

A final kind of anxiety that has received much more attention in recent years is *obsessive-compulsive disorder*. Affecting both sexes equally, it usually begins in adolescence or early adulthood and may affect as many as 2% of the population. OCD, as it is called, involves unrealistic but obsessive worries that constantly intrude upon the child's mind. The most common thoughts involve fear of germs or contamination, an excessive need for order, and recurrent hostile or sexual images. Often these thoughts are then dealt with through compulsions such as repeated hand washing or checking and rechecking locks. These compulsions can begin to take up an amazing amount of time each day.

The bad news is that anxiety problems in adolescence are fairly common. The good news is that they can be successfully treated, often with a combination of education, counseling and medication.

Depression

Depression can also make a teen's life miserable. It involves a persistent mood of sadness or dejection and—like anxiety disorders—usually goes along with low self-esteem. It is common for depressive problems to be accompanied by "biological signs," which include difficulties with eating, sleeping, and energy level. Children and adolescents do not observe and report depression in themselves too well, and it is important to keep in mind that in youngsters this disorder will often manifest itself in a major case of *irritability.*

In what is known as *dysthymic disorder*, the adolescent feels either down in the dumps or irritable most of the time, and to be diagnosed this must have been going on for at least one year. Kids like this don't appear to enjoy things like they used to. They can have difficulty concentrating, and generally feel hopeless and self-critical. Dysthymic disorder will occur at some time or other to approximately 6% of the population and it is two to three times more common in females. It is hard to say what the exact prevalence is in adolescents, because the disorder can begin in childhood, adolescence or early adulthood.

Dysthymia can sometimes lead to *major depressive disorder.* While dysthymic disorder occurs most of the day, more days than not, for a period of at least one year, major depressive disorder involves feeling terribly depressed or irritable all the time for at least two weeks straight. During this time the teen seems to be interested in nothing. They may lose a significant amount of weight, sleep poorly, and be either agitated or excessively fatigued. Indecisiveness, feelings of worthlessness, and suicidal ideas or thoughts about death are also common.

Depressive disorders are also quite treatable with a combination of psychotherapy and medication. Many of the newer antidepressants are remarkable in the effects they can produce, and what is known as "cognitive therapy" can help a lot with self-esteem.

Attention Deficit Disorder

Attention Deficit Disorder (ADD) has received a good amount of attention itself recently. Also referred to as Attention Deficit/Hyperactivity Disorder (ADHD), it probably affects about 3-5% of our adolescents. It also has a hereditary link (it is not caused by bad parenting) and is perhaps two to three times more common in boys. ADD does not start suddenly when a child becomes an adolescent. It is there from the beginning, and often starts causing trouble when the child is just a toddler. ADD is also not outgrown. About 70% of our ADD teens will go on to be ADD adults.

The core symptom of ADD is, of course, a difficulty concentrating that is not caused by another psychological disorder (such as anxiety or depression). In children and adolescents, there are two kinds of ADD: ADD *with* hyperactivity and ADD *without* hyperactivity. In ADD with hyperactivity the concentration problem is accompanied by two other things: a lot of motor activity and a lot of impulsive behavior. The child may have difficulty sitting still and is always on the go. They may also repeatedly blurt things out in class without raising their hand or push another child down when they get angry.

ADD kids like this also show signs such as emotional overarousal, silliness and bossiness in social situations, difficulty following rules, difficulty waiting for something they want, and general disorganization and forgetfulness. Some people say that all kids are like that, but ADD kids show these signs *more often* and at an *inappropriate age*, i.e., they act as if they were three years younger than they really are.

One thing that has complicated the diagnosis of ADD with hyperactivity in adolescents is the fact that by the time they get to be teenagers, many of these kids *move around less*. They are, in other words, less hyper, but they will still be inattentive and emotionally "wired." This is why in the past people used to think ADD would be outgrown, because the most obvious symptom, hyperactivity, often diminished in adolescence.

In ADD without hyperactivity, a major concentration problem exists, but the child may have an average or even placid temperament. These kids don't run around too much, get too excited, or try to push others around (some people feel, however, that they may still sometimes be too impulsive). They do, however, have a difficult time in school and never seem to finish anything. They can be amazingly forgetful and their disorganization can drive their parents crazy.

An interesting thing about ADD without hyperactivity is that many of these children are females. There are many adolescent ADD girls who have spent their lives being disorganized, underachieving in school, and being accused of having little motivation. They didn't receive the appropriate assistance primarily because they didn't cause enough trouble (like many ADD boys do) to call attention to themselves.

Unfortunately, Attention Deficit Disorder doesn't always come by itself. In adolescence as many as 40-50% of ADD kids may also qualify for conduct disorder (see below). Another group of ADD kids—30-40%—may have *learning disabilities*, which can cause them special problems with certain tasks or subject areas even though they have average intelligence.

ADD can usually be managed with what is called "multimodal treatment." That means a combination of education about ADD, parent training in behavior management, counseling, appropriate school interventions, and medication. Approximately 80% of ADD kids will have a good response to one stimulant medication or another. And, contrary to one popular myth, they take the medication throughout their teen years and into adulthood if necessary.

Conduct Disorder

Conduct disorder (CD) is kind of the modern, psychological name for what used to be called juvenile delinquency. Its onset can be as early as six years, but it rarely starts after sixteen years of age. Here the child's behavior is characterized by a repeated violation of the rights of other people and by disregard of age-appropriate norms or rules. These children are often bullies and often get into fights. They can be physically cruel to other people, as well as to animals. They might steal directly from someone, force someone into sexual activity, set fires, and destroy property.

Many parents will find themselves wondering if their child has any conscience at all if they are behaving like this on a regular basis. It is true that conduct disordered adolescents are less capable of sympathy or compassion for others. If they do show remorse, it is often faked in order to avoid punishment. They will often see the intentions of others as hostile—when they are in fact not—and then respond with aggressive behavior. Although they usually have an exterior of defiance or toughness, their self-esteem is usually low.

Keep in mind that these troublesome behaviors must be persistent, not isolated examples, for us to worry about true conduct disorder.

Some people think that the prevalence of CD has increased in recent years and that it is also higher in urban locations. Studies have shown that for persons under eighteen years old, 6% to 16% of males and 2% to 9% of females may qualify for CD. The good news is that the majority of these kids will no longer show these behaviors in adulthood. On the other hand, a large enough proportion will go on to "graduate" to be Antisocial Personality Disorder in adults. This diagnosis exists in approximately 3% of adult males and 1% of adult females.

Although it is common for most teens to experiment with drugs and alcohol during their adolescent years, the incidence of substance abuse in the CD population is much greater than the average and is more likely to persist into adulthood.

Related to and overlapping with CD is *oppositional defiant disorder* (ODD), which is somewhat less serious. It involves persistent patterns of negative and hostile behavior that are characterized by defiant and oppositional reactions toward parents and—often later—other authority figures. These kids just can't seem to do what you want them to! ODD children argue a lot, lose their temper, seem to go out of their way to annoy others, and frequently blame everyone else for their own mistakes. Unlike the conduct disordered children, however, ODD teens are not as aggressive toward others or as destructive.

This pattern of behavior emerges usually at least by early adolescence and it starts most of the time at home. In young children it involves boys more than girls, but in the teen years the sex ratio may be equal. ODD also overlaps with ADD, and it is often a precursor of conduct disorder.

Almost by the very definition of their diagnoses, CD and ODD adolescents are very difficult to treat. They don't take well to therapists (who are authority figures) and don't accept much responsibility for their actions. If ADD coexists with either CD or ODD and the attention deficit can be treated, the prognosis is better. The more aggression there is, the worse the prognosis. One of the most important prognostic indicators for conduct disorder is family stability and consistency of discipline. These kids can get you into war faster than you can think, the Four Cardinal Sins must be avoided like the plague, and misbehavior must be managed as clearly, routinely, and unemotionally as possible. In regard to professional assistance, parents should keep in mind that even if the teen refuses to get involved and see someone, Mom and Dad may still benefit from going themselves and learning how to best manage the difficult situation.

No small task with CD and ODD teenagers, who are often among the most obnoxious of human beings!

Eating Disorders

Eating disorders have also drawn more attention in recent years, and they affect many adolescent girls. They are problems that affect self-esteem immensely, and they are usually not talked about openly. The two most common kinds of problems here are *anorexia nervosa* and *bulimia nervosa*.

Anorexia affects about 1% of the adolescent population and often starts during the teen years. Many writers feel that this estimate is low, or at least that there are many more young girls who are borderline anorexics. It is true that during adolescence, 90% to 95% of girls will diet at some time or another. Anorexia, however, involves the persistent inability or refusal to maintain an appropriate body weight. The girl, in fact, maintains an intense fear of gaining weight, even though her body weight is already low. An anorexic teen cannot see her body as it really is, and she often sees fat where there isn't any. Many girls who have starved themselves for long enough will stop having their periods. The long-term mortality rate for anorexia is approximately 10%, resulting from starvation suicide, or electrolyte imbalances.

With bulimia, which usually begins in late adolescence or early adulthood, the adolescent engages in periodic, secret episodes of binge eating. The amount of food consumed during a binge is often incredible, and it usually involves sweet, high-calorie foods. The binge usually lasts two hours or less, and is then frequently followed by "purging." This is most often done by induced vomiting (or sometimes with laxatives), which reduces the physical discomfort and also the fear of gaining weight. Bulimics, therefore, are often able to maintain a normal weight, but at a high price to their physical and psychological welfare.

Both anorexia and bulimia are very difficult—but not impossible—to treat. The earlier they are diagnosed, the better the prognosis. Some young women also seem to alternate between the two disorders. Group treatment has been found helpful, especially in dealing with the shame and self-hatred that often accompanies an eating disorder. Medications have also helped when there is an accompanying mood disorder, but there is some indication that some antidepressant medications may also help the hunger satiation mechanism in the brain function more normally.

Alcohol and Drug Abuse

The thought of teenagers using alcohol and drugs is frightening to all parents. Parents realize that many adolescents are going through a difficult time in their lives, and unfortunately these substances can be seen by the kids as short-term responses to anger, anxiety and depression as well as other upsets. They can also serve the purpose of making social interactions seem easier, and, in fact, kids who do use drugs regularly tend to hang out together. It is also disconcerting that drug use seems to be modeled for the youngsters by movies, television, professional athletes, and, of course, even by parents themselves.

Studies have indicated that by the time they are seniors in high school, about 90% of all teens will have tried alcohol and about two-thirds will have been drunk at least once. Two-thirds will have tried smoking cigarettes and about 50% or so will have at least experimented with marijuana. One-sixth will have tried inhalants, one-tenth hallucinogens, and a little less than 10% cocaine.

This sounds in a way like adolescents are drug crazy, but this is not the case. Many of these kids learn directly from their own drug use that it is not for them, and they discontinue or temper these activities. Others, however, continue using alcohol or drugs at more dangerous levels. Approximately 15% of high school students may fall into this high-risk group. The largest category here is the multi-drug users, who may use both alcohol and other drugs frequently. Other high-risk groups include the heavy drinkers by themselves (little or no other drugs), consistent users of marijuana, and frequent abusers of stimulants.

What warning signs would you look for if you are concerned about your teenager abusing alcohol or drugs? Sometimes it's very difficult to tell, and sometimes it's not. Keep in mind that many of these kids who are high-risk drug users also qualify for conduct disorder, which we discussed above, which means they may be acting out in many ways. Other indicators include the obvious signs of acute intoxication (such as slurred speech, mental confusion, and glazed or dull eyes), the teen's going through large amounts of money with nothing to show for it, sudden negative changes in behavior (e.g., grades, social life, sleep), moodiness, increased secretiveness and withdrawal, and hanging out with friends whom you either never meet or of whom you have good reason to be suspicious.

If you suspect a drug problem, it's time to talk things over with a professional, even if your teen doesn't at first accompany you.

Divorce Related Problems

Divorce can affect children in a number of ways, not all of which, of course, are bad. One of the most difficult is the loss of the parent who leaves the house—usually the father. Although the harm done is usually worse the younger the child is, teens can also be profoundly affected. They often have had to endure the daily trauma of the pre-divorce marital conflict, and in these situations may feel some relief from the separation of their parents. If they have gotten along best, however, with the parent who leaves the house, and if they don't get along with the one remaining, their daily existence will be more difficult.

Another divorce related problem for adolescents is the difficulty they have in "blended" families. Unfortunately, when there is a remarriage and adolescents are involved, "blended" is often a euphemism for "nothing but trouble." The fact of the matter is that teens don't blend as well as the younger children, and this is usually aggravated the longer the time has been between the divorce and the second marriage. Many adolescents have an extremely difficult time accepting the new step-parent, and some, in fact, never do. Even worse, some new couples are convinced that the teen is deliberately trying to break up the new marriage.

This may not be far from the truth in many situations. Sometimes parents are well-advised to not remarry until the kids are grown and out of the house. What the parents often miss behind the child's constant irritability and lack of cooperation, however, is the pain the youngster feels and their sense of alienation from both of their biological parents as well as from the new parent.

Sexual Abuse

It has been only recently that the problem of sexual abuse of children has received the attention it needs. Although estimates of the prevalence of the problem vary widely, many experts now believe that by the time they are eighteen, at least one out of three females will have been the victim of rape, incest, or molestation by a nonfamily member. The vast majority of the victims are girls, and the vast majority of the perpetrators are males. The trauma to the victim depends upon many factors, including the nature of the assault, the degree of force used, whether the offender was a stranger or familiar, the amount of pain involved, and the length of time the abuse went on and the extent to which intimidation was used to maintain secrecy.

Making matters worse is the conclusion of some researchers that three-fourths of parents who have good reason to suspect abuse either is occurring or has occurred do not report it. The subject is one people do not like to look at or talk about, and confronting it is always traumatic for everyone involved.

The effects of sexual abuse, however, are many and they are often serious. Physical troubles can include chronic pelvic pain, asthma, digestive difficulties, stomachaches, pseudo-seizures, aggravated PMS, and generalized physical complaints. Psychological difficulties can involve depression, increased suicidal risk, bulimia, substance abuse, and sexual disorders.

Children who have been recently abused may show changes in their normal behavior, including sleep disturbances, drop in appetite, regressive behaviors, and exaggerated fears. Some may run away from home (if incest is involved), while others may not want to go out of the house. Some kids may show a sudden interest in sex or get involved in precocious sexual activity.

Long-term effects of sexual abuse often include problems with trust and intimacy, lowered self-esteem, suppressed rage, and a tendency to choose partners who are themselves degrading or abusive. Girls who are victims of incest are often caught between feeling angry about what happened and—surprisingly—feeling guilty and responsible for it. They have more difficulty trusting authority figures. After all, they have been betrayed by one of the ones closest to them.

Abuse can make a girl's life one of unending misery. Professional intervention is necessary, and it should be done with a therapist who knows how to handle this kind of problem. Most often—since most victims are female—the most effective therapist will also be a female. Group therapy is strongly recommended by many experts, but many feel that individual sessions should be done in the beginning.

Finding a Therapist

The problem list above certainly does not include all possible problems that adolescents can run into, only some of the more common ones. Other difficulties teens experience can include psychosis (such as schizophrenia), sexual or gender problems, physical abuse and manic-depressive illness. A good rule of thumb is this: if you have been persistently worried for longer than six months about the possibility of a psychological problem in your son or daughter, you have waited too long. Find someone you trust and get an opinion.

Unfortunately, counselors vary a lot in their approaches and personalities, so you may need to shop around some. Getting an initial referral from a friend, doctor, or local mental health center may be a good way to start. Don't use the yellow pages. Call several counselors, briefly describe the situation, and see how you like them over the phone. If they don't want to give you a few minutes, forget them.

When discussing the possibility of counseling with an adolescent, never say, "You need help," or "We're going to get you some help." The word "help" is a sure way to turn anyone off, and no teen wants to see a shrink in the first place. Instead, you have a couple of other choices for how to bring it up, depending on what kind of relationship you have with the teen.

If your relationship isn't so hot, you might put it something like this, "We are doing a lousy job of working out these problems ourselves, so I think we'll see someone and get their opinion about what to do." Don't argue about it, just set up the appointment.

If you are primarily concerned about the teen—whatever your relationship is like—you had best be honest. "I'm worried about how you're feeling. Lately you don't seem to be yourself at all—too down, having no fun, sleeping too much, and much more irritable. I'm going to ask you to talk to somebody, and maybe we will too."

Sooner or later, most kids will go. If the child refuses to go, you might want to go yourself first and ask the counselor what to do, though it is preferable with teenagers for the child to be seen before the parents. If the teen continues to refuse, you might use the Major/Minor System. For example, "You won't use the car again until you see the counselor at least for the evaluation." Hospitalization might also be considered if the problem is bad enough.

One doctor who often referred people to other professionals suggested a good rule of thumb in selecting a counselor: remember that you are the consumer with the power of choice, and if you have seen someone two times and still don't like them, go find someone else.

Hospitalization

If your situation combines problem kids and bad relationships, sometimes more drastic measures are temporarily required. Legally you have the power to hospitalize your child, if the problems are serious enough and you find a doctor who agrees with you. Physical violence, suicidal behavior, running away, and illegal drug use can all be justifications for temporary hospitalization. Sometimes, police or ambulance services can actually physically transport an unwilling teen to the facility. This is obviously traumatic for all involved, but at times, it's the best choice. It is extremely expensive, however, though insurance often helps cover it.

Your power to hospitalize your child can also be used as leverage in getting them to cooperate with negotiating. Never use it as an empty threat, however. If you threaten it, you'd better have good reason and be ready to do it. Before you even mention it, it's a good idea to have already talked out the reason and the procedure with a professional. Also, look for a mental health professional who will continue to see you after the child is discharged, rather than referring you to someone else and breaking the continuity of the treatment.

Some kids say they'll run away if hospitalization is brought up, and this throws many parents for a loss. This is testing tactic #3, Threat, and if a teen says he's going to do it, you might just have to call his bluff. It's never good to give in to this threat and back down, and it's also not a good idea to try to physically restrain him.

Instead, remember that by far most "runaways" are trips to friends' houses—sort of extended overnights without permission. You can wait for awhile to see if the kid returns, and then call the police. When the child returns or is found, hospitalization may be appropriate. With physical violence, leave the situation or let the child leave, and then consider calling the police for protection or help.

One of the problems with hospitalization is that the child can't stay there forever. You'd go broke long before. Sooner or later, the adolescent has to return to the big, bad world, and most often back home. The same problems will have to be addressed. At best, hospitalization can be a genuine attempt at a new beginning; at worst, it is merely a brief respite from hell.

What if nothing works? You've been through therapy, maybe even with hospitalization, but the kid's still doing horribly, the relationship is a solid 1, and you're going downhill yourself. It may be time to give up on living together.

Don't Live Together

When it comes time to seriously consider not living together, everyone feels a sense of failure. The "rulebook" in our heads says that families are supposed to stay together, that they are supposed to like one another, and that they are supposed to get along. It doesn't always happen like that.

But as they say in the "Tough Love" program, parents are people, too, with limited resources, and there's no future in blaming yourself for everything that went wrong in the past. The kids, after all, weren't really putty in your hands, and if they didn't turn out the way you wanted, there were certainly a lot of different reasons.

There are three alternatives as to how not to live together. Unless the child himself chooses to leave (at an appropriate age, of course), these options still represent the director role.

Residential placement

Although this is not usually a realistic alternative, when living at home is an intolerable situation, there are boarding schools and treatment facilities where kids can board. They can cost $15,000 or more, and insurance does not usually cover the expense. Military schools are often considered here and many are adequate. Call and visit anyplace before considering it. Contact a school or local mental health center to get possibilities.

Kick them out of the house

This sounds terrible, of course, and fortunately doesn't happen too often. It is perhaps more difficult emotionally for everyone than residential placement, but for kids over 18, there may come a time when you just can't live together and a live-in treatment facility is not a good idea for financial or other reasons. At this time, too, the "child" is really an adult and will have to be responsible—come hell or high water—for most all of his problems. Especially in situations where the relationships at home are absolutely terrible, this last resort may be best for everyone.

How do you kick a person out of his own house? You don't do it on the spur of the moment during a fight or argument, unless, perhaps, there has been physical violence. What is sometimes done is a different version of the Major/Minor, but where the consequence is having to leave.

You might write a note saying this:

> *Dear Joe,*
>
> *We are having too much difficulty getting along around here. For the next month, we are going to expect the following from you: not coming home after one o'clock any night,*

*no abusive language, no stealing other people's money,
$50 per month rent.*

*If you cannot hold to these rules, we will ask you to
leave the house. You will be given one month to prepare
for this after we give you notice. We will do our best
to be unprovocative and reasonable during this time.*

Your Parents

If the person can stick to the rules fine. If there is a Major infraction, then he is given notice. Some "kids" will get mad at the letter, tear it up, and screw up right away. They are then given notice. Your odds of success here with the letter aren't too good anyway.

What if the son or daughter won't leave? We have sometimes gotten a lawyer who has written a letter to the person informing them that they are of age, they have been asked to leave, and that refusing to do so will be regarded as trespassing. It's no fun—in fact, it's horrible—but it works. It's your house, after all, and you have a right to protest it and those in it for whom you are responsible. Don't goof up the program by arguing or yelling. It's action you want, not words. What if they still don't leave by the time in the letter? Your attorney can instruct you about how the courts and the police can assist you in removing anyone who is illegally in your house.

Living elsewhere

At times situations do occur where the kid (13-18) is not a disaster area, but nevertheless the relationship for some reason stinks. Some of these teens can still get along well with other adults, and so a few families will try to negotiate living arrangements with other relatives or, more rarely, friends. Maybe old Uncle Joe in Michigan's Upper Peninsula needs a little company. Step 3, Negotiating, should be used here as well as it can be with the adolescent and the other family. Ground rules, money, and living arrangements should be made perfectly clear.

Part IV

No Teenager Will Thank You

13

Testing & Manipulation

If you are frustrating someone in some way by not giving them what they want, they have three choices. First, they can decide it's not such a big deal and put up with the frustration. Second, they can make a sincere attempt to negotiate with you. And third, they can try to test or manipulate you.

Behavior with a Purpose

Testing and manipulation is not unusual or sick; it is a normal, aggravating part of family life. Adults do it and kids do it. They do it when they are frustrated and they want to indirectly weasel their way out of something. Your teens will not usually thank you for disciplining them. Instead they will test and manipulate to see how far they can get. You are especially likely to get more testing as you begin doing things that are more intrusive.

Because it occurs when the adolescent is frustrated, testing is purposeful behavior. Actually, it has two possible purposes. *The first purpose of testing and manipulation is for the teenager to get what they want*. Let me go out, don't ask me to do my homework, lend me a few bucks, get off my case.

The second purpose of testing comes into play if the first purpose fails—if the child doesn't get his way he will try to get something else. *The second purpose of T&M is revenge.* They are going to try to make you pay for your insensitivity to their needs.

Being knowledgeable about and prepared for testing and manipulation is critical to successfully parenting your adolescent. It will do no good to put a large amount of careful thought into how to handle a situation if you can't manage the teen's response to what you do. You can't expect your kids to be grateful to you for disciplining or frustrating them. It will most often be true, however, that whenever you use only the observer role, you won't get testing from the kids.

When anybody "decides" to engage in manipulative attempts to influence another person, they have basically six choices: Badgering, Intimidation, Threat, Martyrdom, Butter Up, and Physical Tactics. These things (except for Butter Up) are meant to frustrate the parent in some way. What the frustrated adolescent is implicitly doing, then, is offering you a deal: now that we're both frustrated, you call off your dogs and I'll call off mine.

If you do give them their way, they will often immediately stop whatever testing tactic they were using. If you do this on a regular basis, you can have them running the house in no time.

Tactic 1: Badgering

When using this tactic, our unhappy camper repeatedly harps at you about what they want. Over and over and over. The idea is this: to wear you down; just give me the stupid car or whatever for tonight and I'll leave you alone. It might go something like this:

"Dad, can you loan me five bucks?"
"I just gave you your allowance yesterday."
"It's gone, and we're going out for pizza."
"You should have been more careful."
"Come on, Dad, they're picking me up in five minutes!"
"How many times have I told you to think before blowing all your allowance in one day?"

"The point is they're on their way!"

"What did you do with it?"

"With what? Dad, please—just this once."

"Why don't you ever hit on your mother?"

"That's them! Please—I'll look like an idiot!"

"All right, d—n it, just get off my back!"

Score: Kid 5, Dad 0. Dad was caught off guard, tried unsuccessfully to argue, then became overwhelmed with sympathy.

Tactic 2: Intimidation

The second testing tactic is also aggressive, but it is more vicious than the first. Here the frustrated teen has a temper tantrum, yells, swears, or accuses you of being a lousy parent. The goal, obviously, is to make you feel uncomfortable:

"Mom, can I use your lipstick?"

"You've got some of your own."

"I can't find it."

"Then look around. I'm tired of you using and losing my
  stuff."

"Well thanks one h—l of a lot! One simple, stupid, apparently
  mental, god—n, idiot request and it's too much for precious
  mother. Gosh, the level of caring and consideration for
  others around this hole is overwhelming. I'm fainting from
  too much love! Keep your c—p lipstick and I'll tell you
  what you can do with it!"

Quite nasty, wouldn't you say? Intimidation can inspire extreme anger or extreme fear in a parent. Since it is so unpleasant, it is often hard not to give in to some demand before the child has a chance to go into the fit. The teen asks for something, and immediately you have this uneasy feeling in the pit of your stomach: if you don't give them what they want, all hell will break loose.

Tactic 3: Threat

The third manipulative strategy is Threat. Here the teenage charmer states directly or implies that some untoward consequence will befall you should you continue to refuse to grant their wishes. On the other hand, should you wish to avoid this inevitable tragedy, the solution is clear and readily available.

Fourteen year old Maria wanted to go out to a movie on a school night, but Mrs. Carey said she had to stay home for her usual study time, especially since she had a biology test coming up the next day:

> "Mom, I can study when I get back."
> "It will be time for bed."
> "I won't be able to concentrate with all of them out there
>   having a great time, and me just here doing nothing."
> "Sorry."
> "You'll be sorry when I flunk this test."
> "You'll do OK if you study."
> "I'm too ticked to even think. How am I supposed to concen-
>   trate on that biology? It's garbage."
> "Do the best you can."
> "Can't even do one simple thing. You're gonna regret this—
>   you wanna see a lousy progress report—just wait till
>   midterm..."

Maria threatens to not study, then to flunk the test, then to do poorly in the rest of her courses as well. Some kids go big time and threaten to run away, get pregnant, or kill themselves. The goal of Tactic 3 is to make Mom or Dad anxious. They can then eliminate their anxiety by giving in to their son or daughter.

Tactic 4: Martyrdom

This tactic may be the all time favorite of children and adults. Here the unhappy adolescent pouts, cries, looks sad, doesn't talk, doesn't eat, or otherwise indicates that life has become incredibly burdensome since the advent of the new frustration. The obvious cause of the torture, of course, is Mom or Dad. Conversations with the youngster may disappear completely, while in other cases they may become quite short:

"How was your evening?"
"OK."
"What did you guys do?"
"Nothing."
"You had to do something."
(Silence)

The Silent Treatment. Dad is getting it because he told his daughter she couldn't go to a motel all night after the prom coming up in two weeks.

Martyrdom is obviously designed to make the parent feel guilty, and for many adults this can be a real problem. The tactic is more subtle than Badgering or Intimidation, which are often blatant attempts at manipulation. With Martyrdom the implied message is something like, "Life is hardly worth living since what you've done to me, and you don't deserve to be talked to anymore. But don't worry about me, I'll handle things from now on by myself."

Unfortunately, some parents have a "guilt button" the size of the state of Wyoming, and it is all too easy for other people to press it and get what they want. If this type of parent tries to escape the guilt by giving in, however, they often simply trade their guilt for anger when they realize—once again—that they've been had.

Tactic 4 is sometimes hard to tell from genuine clinical depression. There are differences, though. Depression will be more persistent and will also exist even when the child is not being frustrated by you. Martyrdom will occur from time to time when the child is frustrated. A depressed teen may not enjoy anything. A teen who uses Martyrdom periodically can still enjoy things the rest of the time.

Tactic 5: Butter Up

This testing tactic is different, because it is the only one of the six where the adolescent doesn't make you feel uncomfortable. Here they make you comfortable! Sort of.

With the Butter Up routine the child does something like compliment you, or promise something nice, or complete some rather unusual chore around the house. But there is a catch: you are expected to reciprocate by not frustrating them in some way. If you don't respond correctly, you may observe with fascination (and horror) the immediate transformation of Butter Up to Intimidation:

> "Well I cleaned up the garage. Can I have the car tonight?"
> "I didn't ask you to clean the garage. In fact I just did it last week."
> "Well, there was some junk lying around. What about the car?"
> "Your mother and I need it."
> "For what?"
> "It doesn't make a lot of difference, Brandon, we have to go out."
> "Well thanks a lot. You know, you try to do something nice around here for someone and what happens: you get dumped on!"
> "Watch it, buddy."
> "You watch it! I'm sick and tired of having to stay around here all the time while you guys cover the globe anytime you want. Why the h—l don't you fix that other piece of @#$% in the driveway so I can go out once every year or two!"

Here the token garage cleaning was obviously manipulative and, unlike the other testing tactics, it preceded the frustrating event. Butter Up, however, is often hard to tell from genuine affection or consideration, so you have to evaluate it carefully. In addition, there is certainly nothing wrong with making a deal that if the garage is cleaned, the teen can use the car. This would be true negotiation rather than Butter Up.

Tactic 6: Physical

One of the worst forms of testing and manipulation—and, fortunately, probably the least common, is employing Physical measures to get your way. These include attacking other people, breaking things, and running away. Obviously things can sometimes get pretty scary.

Kids who use Physical tactics often have a history of this kind of thing. Physical tactics are not uncommon, for example, in conduct disordered kids. They don't usually pop up one day on their own. Parents who have encountered it have often become vulnerable to another testing tactic, and that is Threat. The threat of physical harm or damage can certainly make you think twice about sticking to your guns with a kid like this.

14

Managing Testing & Manipulation

M anaging testing and manipulation is not very easy, but it certainly helps if you first recognize testing for what it is. Labelling it in your own mind while it is happening is very helpful. "Oh, there's another example of Martyrdom," or "Here we go again with the Badgering."

Next you must understand the basic principles regarding how T&M works, so you know what to expect. And finally, you need to know exactly what to do and what not to do when confronted with the manipulative efforts of your youngsters.

Some Important Basic Principles

Several basic considerations become apparent when you reflect on the purpose of testing and the different tactics kids can use.

First of all, *if an adolescent frequently repeats one particular form of testing, you probably are not handling it well.* Why? Because people naturally tend to repeat behavior that works for them. Check to see if you are either caving in and giving them what they want, or—even if you don't give in—getting so upset that the teen knows he is getting exquisite,

111

satisfying revenge. Either one will make them want to use the same tactic again.

Second, in the beginning, *as you get better at not giving in, the kids may either escalate one tactic or switch tactics.* The temper tantrums may get worse for a while if you suddenly decide you are no longer giving in to them. Or the adolescent may switch tactics on you, trying to find one that gets through:

> "Can I use the car tonight?"
> "No, I need it."
> "Why not?"
> "Have to go shopping."
> "Can't you do it tomorrow?" (Badgering)
> "No."
> "I'll put some gas in it." (Butter Up)
> "Can't do it."
> "Come on, d——t, just for two hours. Why do you have to be such a pig about it!" (Intimidation)
> "How many times do I have to tell you you can't have it?"
> "See if I'm home when you get back." (Threat)
> "You can go to h——l for all I care."
> "Fine, I'll just sit in this excuse for a house all weekend."
> (Threat/Martyrdom)

This is aggravating and scary, but keep in mind that it is a sign that you are doing better at not giving in all the time.

Third, *never give in after the teen has started testing.* This is a great way to reinforce aggravating behavior. Keep in mind, though, this does not imply you shouldn't grant the kids' requests when you think they're reasonable. If you have doubts, tell your son or daughter to give you a few minutes to think it over, then give them your response. Tell them to be ready either way. If your answer is "No," be prepared for the worst and keep quiet.

Fourth, *if you continue to remain reasonable and firm in handling requests and testing tactics, escalation and switching will decrease over time.* The kids will eventually get more used to it, they will know what their limits are, and—believe it or not—they will be happier. Why? Because almost by definition T&M means they are getting upset too. Both of you will be happier because the frequency, intensity, and duration of hassles will be less.

Exactly how do you handle the little devils' manipulative efforts? We'll get to that in just a minute.

Testing and Manipulation by Parents

Kids, of course, aren't the only ones who are capable of trying roundabout strategies in order to get their way. When they are frustrated or can't seem to get through to their adolescent any other way, Mom and Dad can naturally slip into using some of these tactics themselves.

Badgering. The parent version of this is one of the Four Cardinal Sins, Nagging. When parents do it, it doesn't always have the same urgency as when kids do it, but it's still a form of Badgering. It expresses frustration and the almost psychotic delusion that repetition will solve the problem.

Intimidation. A parental favorite. Yelling and screaming don't really solve much either. They are often a sign of emotional dumping and common when a state of war exists.

Threat. Using this tactic can goof up the Major/Minor System in a big way. You don't want to threaten something that you're not going to do, because you'll begin to lose your credibility. Don't say, "You're not going out tonight if your room isn't clean," if you don't mean it.

Martyrdom. Another parental favorite, especially when parents feel powerless or intimidated by their teens. When you are feeling like nothing else will work, why not try some heavy duty guilt induction? This tactic may be used a little less since the phrase, "guilt trip," became popular, but it still goes on a lot.

Butter Up. Parents—like the kids—don't use this too much. It's often too easy for the adolescents to see through it.

Physical. Mom and Dad don't use this one much either with adolescents. If they do, we may have a problem with child abuse (physical), or Mom or Dad may also get hurt themselves. Normally physical confrontations at home make everyone feel sick.

The 'Guilt vs Anger' Problem

A very common and interesting problem arises in the course of many relationships. It occurs when one person offers another person the choice of feeling angry or feeling guilty. This problem then involves an interaction between two testing tactics: Intimidation (#2) and Martyrdom (#4).

Here's how it goes: 13 year old Kristina walks into the room where her father, Mr. Applegate, is busy watching his favorite football team. With an innocent question, Kristina offers her father the choice of whether he wants to be angry or guilty:

"Dad, can you drive me to Jenny's?"
"Kristina, that's clear across town."
"It will only take forty minutes."
"You know, you pick the worst times to ask me for rides."
"Your stupid football's more important, huh?"
"Why the h—l can't you ever plan ahead?"
"You never do anything with me anyway!"
"OK, OK. Let's move before the d—n game's over."
"No, hate to ruin your day. Thanks anyway—I'll just stay home!"

When his daughter asks him for a ride, Mr. Applegate can either take her, and feel resentful, or he can refuse, and feel guilty. The choice is clear; what to do isn't.

This type of thing occurs frequently in all kinds of relationships. Furthermore, it's interesting that if people have to choose between feeling angry or feeling guilty, they usually prefer anger. Perhaps the reason is that when you are angry, you are thinking someone else messed up, but when you're guilty, you're thinking you screwed up.

Whatever the reason, you often wind up with two people sort of jockeying for position, trying to take the angry position and at the same time put the other person in the guilty role. When Dad says, "You pick the worst times...," or, "OK,OK. Let's move before the game is over," he is saying, "I'll be angry and you be guilty." But Kristina isn't about to stand for this, so she comes back with, "Your stupid football is more important," and "I'll just stay home." If she does stay home, she may become the official winner of this match: she can be angry and Dad will feel guilty.

You're probably thinking, "This sounds pretty stupid." It is, but it happens a lot. Isn't there a more rational solution than two people trying to guilt each other to death? Certainly it would be better to negotiate (or to plan ahead). Perhaps Dad could have responded by saying, "I can take you if you can hold on till halftime," or something like that.

If you are the parent on the receiving end of a spontaneous request like the one above, or in some other situation with your teen that might involve this kind of jockeying, your best bet is to say "no" or make a reasonable counteroffer. Then—if the teen is still unhappy—live with the guilt if you have to, and avoid coming back with Intimidation to eradicate your discomfort (check out Mom's reaction to Deedee in the example coming up).

Managing Testing & Manipulation

Back to testing and manipulation by the teens. Exactly how do you handle it? The answers can be found in the earlier discussions of the Four Cardinal Sins and the Major/Minor System.

For Verbal Tactics (1-4)

For the more verbal tactics, such as Badgering, Intimidation, Threat, and Martyrdom, don't get baited into spontaneous discussions, arguing, or lectures (you usually won't have to worry about your nagging because the teenager will be doing the nagging). There may come a time in the conversation when you have to just shut up, even if your offspring is still going at it. You may even have to leave the room. You may have to just stand there—saying nothing—while you keep doing the dishes. It doesn't feel very good, but there's no point in talking anymore.

Mom does a good job in this example:

"Deedee, your clothes aren't down here for the wash."
"Can you get them for me?"
"No, I can't."
"Mom, I'm right in the middle of this show!"
(Silence)

"Give me a break, will ya!"

"Sorry."

"Oh for pete's sake, I gotta do everything around here." (Goes
   to get clothes)

(Silence)

It's very hard not to get tricked here into some lecture about
responsibility or about who really does all the work around here, but in this
interchange Mom is the model of self-restraint.

For Abusive Verbal or Physical Tactics

For more drastic verbal and for Physical testing tactics, the Major/Minor
System can be invoked. Things such as swearing, big time name calling,
staying out late, or smashing household goods require consequences.
Look back at our Major, Medium, and Minor categories and decide which
would be appropriate. Words by themselves seldom merit a Major
consequence, but breaking things might and physically hurting someone
else would. If a child is doing this kind of thing on a regular basis, some
kind of professional evaluation might also be in order.

For both repeated minor as well as major episodes of testing,
sometimes it is helpful to use negotiating. Here the problem being
discussed is testing itself. In counseling sessions we have had some very
interesting conversations about this. First we show the kids and the parents
the list of six tactics in SYA. Then we ask the teens: "Which ones are your
favorites and which are your parents' favorites?" Next we ask the parents
the same question in reverse. If you try this with your children, be ready
to admit that you are not perfect either and may use a little T&M from time
to time. Don't try to have this discussion on the spur of the moment, of
course.

Living with teens on a regular, day-to-day basis, you must always be
prepared to handle one or more of the six tactics. If you are not, you are
engaging in wishful thinking and simply setting yourself up for trouble.

When confronted with testing, have you ever said, "Why can't you
ever take 'No' for an answer?", "I'm sick and tired of your hassling me all

the time," or "You're never happy unless you get your way, are you?"?

It's almost as if parents who say these things are expecting their kids to appreciate their efforts to raise them and to be thankful for any discipline provided. Get a life!

And be prepared.

Part V

Managing Specific Problems

15

Guidelines for Specific Problems

B elow are some suggestions, using the ideas in ***Surviving Your Adolescents***, for handling the problems originally listed in the Preface. What is suggested will sometimes vary depending on the age of the teen and your overall feeling about their competence. If you already have a good solution, forget the advice in ***SYA*** and stick with yours. These ideas are only suggestions, not rules.

Arguing

This is the #1 problem parents of adolescents complain about. What these parents often forget is that they control 50% of an argument, since it always takes two people to produce one. Many times arguments continue because each person has to have the last word. Mathematically speaking, if you have two people arguing, and each insists on having the last word, you have a potentially infinite discussion. Ad nauseam.

Arguing shouldn't happen if you are studiously avoiding the Four Cardinal Sins. Arguing is useless and provocative. Sometimes active listening can help abort an argument, then negotiating might prove useful if there is a problem that needs to be resolved. If you're getting yourself too angry, cool off and think before trying to talk again. If you are regularly having too much trouble keeping quiet, you are probably doing a lot of emotional dumping

Arguments will rarely help to get your point across. Say what you have to, if necessary, then drop it. Remember that in the entire history of parenting, no teenager has ever responded to a parental tirade with a sincere, "Gee, I never looked at it like that before."

Bedtime

For the younger 13-15 year old adolescent group, if there is a problem, the best method is simple advice, especially for competent or even average kids. If the problem persists, negotiating may be the next logical step. If the child, however, persists in going to bed ridiculously late, or bothering other family members, the Major/Minor may have to be used. Some really weird sleeping schedules can be related to drug use or depression, so this sometimes needs to be evaluated if the problem continues in spite of everything.

For older teens, even problem kids, stay out of it unless the child is disturbing others at night or the teen's sleeping schedule is just too unorthodox. Problem children will probably have other more important difficulties that you need to worry about.

Bumming around town

Or shopping malls. This area is controversial, but we suggest giving the kids some leeway. During the day or early evening, letting average to competent 13-15 year olds hang around malls or downtown areas is fine. Ask them to tell you where they are going. Some parents require a call if the kids change places, but this is a request that is difficult for most teens to comply with. It's probably best not to insist on a call, unless the kids want to go someplace far or risky.

Violations or getting in trouble while bumming around are handled with the Major/Minor System—usually some kind of grounding. Repeated problems require a renegotiation of the whole idea of their going out like that.

Older kids can tell you where they think they are going and that's it.

No calls are necessary unless they are going out of state or something. Parties would be covered by the rules agreed upon for that (see Parties: home and away), and hours must be respected (see Hours). Don't grill them: "Where are you going, with whom, what are you going to do, who's idea was that, what if this happens, how much money do you have, where's your coat it's cold out there and I think you're catching a cold," etc.

What about kids who have already been having problems with this? If they've already been getting into trouble with bumming around, they don't go for a while. Then try giving them some rope, and if they goof up, it's grounding time for a short, defined period, then try it again. One thing here that's hard is shutting up and not grilling them before they go out. You are anxious and you want some reassurance, but you will just irritate them with all your questions. Now we have an Irritated Problem Kid going out for a while, and that's worse. If you want, they can tell you where they are going and whom they will be with, and that's it.

Car: care, use, gas

There are many arrangements possible. For more competent teenagers, free use (if there are enough cars) is reasonable, and the child pays either all or half the gas. Average to competent kids could even buy their own car, provided they pay the insurance and their grades stay good. Many insurance companies have 25% discounts for kids who maintain a B average in school. Some families have the adolescent pay the extra if they don't keep the B average. Don't do this, though, unless you're sure that your son or daughter is capable of that kind of schoolwork in the first place.

Hooking up car use to grades is fine as long as the deal is defined precisely. For example, the teen can use the car whenever they wish, provided they maintain a C+ average (2.75 on a 4 point system) with no F's for any quarter or progress report. If they drop below this, the use of the car is restricted temporarily (define the time) until they get back to 2.75. If you have a difficult child with marginal school performance, no car on week nights (unless rare special occasions) is a good idea. No drinking and driving, and hours must be respected.

Care of the car (changing oil, checking tires, etc.) is something of a problem, because many kids just don't know much about it to begin with.

Dad usually winds up taking care of it, which is fine. If the child is interested and wants to learn, negotiating the deal would certainly be a good idea.

Chores

Negotiating is probably the best place to start with chores. Attempts at advice too often turn into nagging. Sit everyone in the family down, divide the chores up, and if you want, hook up some of the allowance to the chore (you have to keep track of who did what). *Avoid making spontaneous requests about chore-like tasks.* Parents are always saying things like, "I only asked you to do one little thing, what's the big deal?" The big deal is that everyone—including parents—hates to be interrupted.

"But he never does anything he's supposed to!" Some kids are just naturally forgetful. Nagging won't help, but if you don't do something, you'll feel angry and martyrlike. A good option is the "Docking" system, which was discussed before as a version of the Major/Minor System. You have a problem with Mike feeding the dog regularly in the evening and he had agreed to do it (Mike is 14 and gets an allowance of $8). Simply tell him the dog should be fed by 6 PM. If the dog isn't fed, you will do it. But, you charge 50¢ to do a feeding. If you don't get to it right at 6:05 and Mike beats you to it, there's still no charge. No reminders! You can use the same procedure for laundry, dishes, and cleaning the house.

Many parents find it easier to just do things around the house themselves. That way things get done, and they get done right, right? There's probably nothing horribly wrong with this, but you have to be careful you don't become a Major Martyr and then expect everyone else to respond with enthusiasm to your requests for "help" on the spur of the moment.

Church

If you haven't done much about attending church before, you're probably not going to start when your kids are age 13 or more. Modeling is important here: you can't expect them to go much if you don't. For 13-15 year olds, your involvement here is optional and it depends a lot upon what your religious beliefs are. It probably isn't a good idea to go past negotiating for a child who is giving you a hard time by not attending church. Grin and Bear It, and keep quiet about it on Sunday mornings.

For 16-18 year olds, staying out is the best bet, perhaps after one shot at consulting. For some people, having their child talk to their pastor or minister alone has been more helpful than the teen talking to his parents. Many times if the kids talk to someone outside the family, they are on their best behavior and also are much more reasonable.

Clothes, hair, earrings

This is true MBA territory. *Keep in mind that for many adolescents their appearance is designed to look weird and to shock you.* If you have a fit about it, you're playing right into their hands.

With any teens, the best advice is probably to tell the kids that they can wear anything the school will let him in the door with. This isn't necessarily saying a lot, because schools these days will put up with some pretty horrendous outfits. The farthest you should go in most situations is just giving advice. Otherwise Grin and Bear It. Even if your son comes home with a huge, colored, dangling earring.

However, you would not want to allow your child to wear a T-shirt to a wake. Some kids have tried it! But you also can't dress them. If necessary, give some advice or try talking it over in situations like this. If all else fails, don't sit with him, don't let anyone else know he's yours, let him stay home, or treat it as a Minor infraction.

But remember: "Styles change, Mom!" If the adolescent's wearing something really weird, try to deawfulize it and keep in mind that they very likely won't be dressing like that ten years from now. With difficult kids, in addition, you certainly don't need any extra hassles over something nonessential.

If the school is actually not letting the child in the door because of dress, that's a different story. You certainly should consider going to the Major/Minor System. It must be quite an outfit!

If you've already had a set of rules for hairstyles and dress, and your adolescents are used to them, forget the advice here and keep doing what you're already doing.

College plans

For these older adolescents, advisor and negotiator roles are appropriate. You, after all, most likely have to pay for room and board and tuition, or at least for a lot of it. Tell them what your financial limits are and look at some possible schools together. It's amazing how many parents seem to just let their son or daughter pick a school, then Mom and Dad try to figure out a way to pay for it. When their relationship with you is fairly good, many kids need and appreciate advice, direction, and support.

Depression

Genuine depression is always a serious problem. It can also run in families, so family history is important to pay attention to. Other signs of depression include:

1. Pervasive gloom
2. Difficulty enjoying anything
3. Irritability
4. Low self-esteem
5. School underachievement
6. Social withdrawal
7. Appetite disturbance
8. Sleeping disturbance
9. Being slowed down or tired all the time

If you feel you have a depressed teenager, it's time to consult a professional. This is nothing for you to try to diagnose or deal with yourself.

Drugs and drinking

For 13-15 year olds, drinking and drug use are out. If necessary, start with the Major/Minor method. But feel free to go right on to Evaluation and Counseling, or even Hospitalization if needed. Outpatient drug and alcohol programs are easy to find these days, and are often connected to hospitals.

Education is very helpful. Educate yourself and then discuss (not lecture) the matter with your child. If you're not sure if there is a problem, or you're not sure what to do, call one of the outpatient counselors. They are usually very helpful. A counselor can tell you some of the things to look for if you're suspecting substance abuse in your child. They can also tell you about the nature and cost of an evaluation, about urine testing, and about what to do if the teen refuses to cooperate with anything you do. Remember, you have the legal right to hospitalize your child under 18 if there is sufficient cause.

With kids 16-18, drinking is still illegal, but some families allow an occasional beer or glass of wine at home provided there is no driving afterwards. Violations with drugs or alcohol are considered Medium to Major offenses, and are dealt with accordingly.

Family outings

The problem is that a lot of times teens don't want to go with you anymore when you are going out as a family. This is perfectly normal. For 13-15 year olds, working out some kind of a deal may be a good idea, because you may not want to leave them home alone. Punishment for not going may at times be appropriate, but you'll usually have a sullen kid on your hands if you force them to go. Consider doing nothing, leave them home, and enjoy yourself!

For older teens, they can decide for themselves if they want to go with you. There shouldn't be much problem leaving them home by themselves. If they goof up when you're gone (like having a huge, wild party at your house), of course, you'd use the Major/Minor program.

Friends and dating

With friends we suggest staying out at all ages. This is a definite advisor role if you don't like the other adolescent, although you might try negotiating (if you listen first). Part of the problem here is that it is next to impossible to control—especially with older teens who drive whom your child sees out of the house. In addition, with poor parent/child relationships, your trying to stop a relationship with one of their undesirable friends may only serve to make it stronger.

If you can stand it, invite the other creep over to your house and see if you can get along. Some of them aren't so bad! If the other child is, in fact, a bad influence, you certainly can use the Major/Minor System on your child for whatever trouble he gets into. In desperate situations, you might actually use the Major/Minor for merely getting together with a certain other teenager if you are sure they are having a very bad effect.

Many parents don't let their kids date until they're 16 years old. Others let the child date, but not alone in a car until they're 16. Parents can chauffeur, or the kids can go out in groups. Violations are handled by the Major/Minor System. It's certainly a good idea, if your teen is going out on a date, to meet the other party beforehand or at the earliest possible time.

Grades and homework

With competent children and temporary drops in grades, merely watching and doing some listening might be all that is necessary. Negotiating a positive reward system (like money for grades) has been used with success to help wake the kids up, but the Major/Minor System by itself is not always so useful since it involves only punishment. "You're grounded until you get those grades up!" is a message that, if used, needs to be much more specific (e.g., 2.50 GPA with no F's), and that also needs some positive reinforcement attached to it.

Negotiating set study hours—with no phone interruptions allowed—is often helpful for kids who are struggling. Believe it or not, many adolescents can study better with their radios on (it blocks out other distracting noises), but never with the TV.

Try not to be checking the child's work all the time, but if you insist on this perverse procedure, be sure to use a lot of positive reinforcement and don't insist on perfection. Tell them if they did something *right* on any of their assignments, for pete's sake! Hooking up the use of the car, as well as more freedom during the week, with a periodic, specifically defined grade check can also work, provided you don't argue about it. It is also a good idea to write the deal down on paper.

If all this fails, a professional evaluation, and perhaps psychological testing, may be necessary. Coming up with a diagnosis of learning disability, Attention Deficit Disorder, or something else may shed light on the situation, even though there's already a lot of water under the bridge.

Grammar

It's a little late.

Hours

Hours should be clear for all ages, though for kids in the 16-18 group who are generally doing well, considerable flexibility is OK, as long as it's not abused.

For kids aged 13-15, staying in on week nights during the school year is a good idea for average to difficult kids, unless there is some special reason to go out. With competent kids, going out is not a problem, and you might use the bumming around suggestions above.

What hours are reasonable? We usually suggest sticking with curfew pretty strictly, with some leeway for competent 16-17 year olds. This often means something like 11 PM on Sunday through Thursday and 12 midnight on Friday or Saturday.

What about violations? For first time offenses, just give them some friendly advice. With continued problems, however, a handy and simple system is the following:

1. 15 minutes late grace period.
2. After 15 minutes late, the child must "pay back" the minutes next time he goes out—he must come in that much earlier.
3. After 45 minutes late, he must pay back double time.
4. After three hours late, one week grounding or consider it a Major.

No grilling when the adolescent comes in: "Where were you?", "Why can't you ever get home on time?", etc. You may just be asking for a lot of lies or other forms of verbal refuse, and it makes it harder for everyone to get to sleep afterwards.

Music

Trying to control the quality or nature of the music the children listen to is probably a lost cause. Trying to deal with its volume may not be.

However, if you are strange enough yourself that you too can enjoy their musical preferences, no problem.

Advice can get real tedious here and quickly becomes nagging: "Turn that d—n thing down!" If you don't like this form of noise pollution, negotiate something like sharing the cost of earphones or some other solution. They have to turn it down only when someone else is home, for example. If that doesn't work, small fines can, and if that fails, temporary removal of the stereo (e.g., one day removal after three unsuccessful warnings in one day) follows.

Meals and eating habits

Rigid adherence to attendance at nightly family dinners is less and less appropriate as the child gets older. Suggesting making four of seven each week, for example, or negotiating something else is more reasonable, but it's not worth a Major/ Minor. It might be better to go back to merely being an observer. Nagging about coming to the dinner table is not allowed, no matter what you cooked.

What the child eats should be handled the same way. Suggesting taking three of the four foods available often works well, but if the teen wants something else, the answer is either "No" or "You'll have to get it (and maybe pay for it) yourself."

Sloppy eating habits have never been nagged away. Try some friendly advice. If that fails, don't eat together. Attendance at meals and manners are not earthshaking problems, and with problem children trying to do something about them is often more trouble than it's worth.

Messy rooms

Close the door and don't look. This is perhaps the all-time, classic MBA. It's their territory, and there is no research demonstrating a relation between sloppy rooms in childhood and lack of success or criminal activity in adulthood. Two problems here: dirty dishes and laundry. If they don't get their laundry down to the washing machine once a week, it doesn't get washed, or they do it themselves. If you have to pick up dirty dishes from the pig sty, just charge them 10 cents per and forget about it.

Money, allowance, loans

Allowances are helpful for two reasons: they can be used as incentives for chores and things, and they can be handy when fines or the Docking System are used (such as for swearing), and you would like total control over the consequences.

How much is reasonable? Who knows? But here are some guidelines: for 13-15 year olds, about $4-8; 16-18 year olds, $8-12 or so. Consider continuing the allowance even if they get a job (you may need some clout).

It's preferable not to get involved in how the adolescent spends his money. Let them learn through trial and error the benefits of saving or restraining their impulsivity. Some families, where the kids will eventually go to college, require that the child save one half of all earnings for the college fund. If you've already been doing this, keep it up if it's working.

If you are not telling them how to spend their money, you are also not going to regularly provide "loans" to bail them out when they're short. If loan requests are rare, there's no problem with helping them out. But when it becomes a regular thing, these so called loans actually will become gifts, and you will be subsidizing irresponsibility.

If you do make loans, keep them small and set up a strict payback schedule. Make sure it's clear to begin with if the money is a loan or a gift, and don't make additional loans until the first one is paid back. If the kid is defaulting, garnish the allowance.

Negative attitude

Some kids, it seems, were born crabby. They just appear to always be in a bad mood or to have a chip on their shoulder. Many other people—adults included—are generally in good spirits, except for the morning.

Often one of the worst things you can do is try to cheer up one of these non-morning people. Your "Isn't this going to be a nice day!" at 6:50 AM will be met with the unprintable. So leave them alone.

If the negative attitude is something new and it persists, it may be a good idea to consider some gentle active listening, or even professional counseling if it seems serious enough. Remember that in kids continued irritability is frequently a sign of depression. Never chase a martyr, however. If the teen is nonverbally "broadcasting" that he is upset about something, and your "What's wrong?" questions are always met with "Nothing," you are stuck. Instead, say "It looks like something's on your mind. If you want to talk about it, let me know." Then turn around and walk away.

Parties: home and away

For 13-15 year olds, no problem if you're there. For 16-18 year olds, you might allow a party if you're not home only for competent kids, good parent/child relationships, and very limited numbers. Use negotiating first to clarify ground rules, and don't go too far away! Explain to the kids what to do if the party gets out of hand (like call the police), then ask them if they would really do it.

No drinking is allowed. If you are there, anyone who drinks turns in their car keys upon arriving and spends the night. If you find out later that someone is drinking, they also spend the night. If your own party is crashed by too many people and you can't handle it, call the police. If you've had repeated problems with parties in the past, just say "No," explain once, and prepare for testing.

Kids any age can be allowed to go to a party where the parents are home. With difficult kids and bad parent/child relationships, call beforehand to make sure the parents will be there. Expect flak from your child about this, and comments like, "All my friends think you guys are weird."

If the parents aren't home, 13-15 year olds don't go. If they told you the parents would be there and they misled you, consult with the teen the first time, then treat it as a Medium offense afterwards.

With 16-18 year olds, competent kids might be allowed to go to parties where parents aren't home, provided there is no trouble. Some parents forget here that for many teens, exposure to drug or alcohol use winds up turning them off instead of tempting them. If you're not sure what your child's reaction would be to this, sit down sometime, ask them, and do your best to listen.

If they get in hot water, use the Major/Minor after the first offense. Their activities are cut back for two weeks to one month, then let them try it again after some negotiation and advice.

Problem kids don't go to parties where the parents aren't home. If they do it's a Major. There's too much chance for trouble. If they accuse you of not trusting them, tell them nicely that they are correct.

Phone

As all parents of adolescents know, phones are obnoxious devices that we could all live better without. In order to help magnify this curse, however, modern technology has also provided us with the benefits of Call Waiting, answering machines, and 900 numbers that "instruct" the kids not to listen if they're under 18.

Incoming calls you pretty much have to put up with, but a negotiated or imposed rule about no incoming calls after 10 PM or so is reasonable. The kids can tell their friends to cool it after a certain time.

If most of the calls coming in are for your kids, don't answer the phone yourself. It's a waste of time.

If the phone bill is too high, some families have the kids share the cost. If the kids get their own phone, they ideally should pay for it themselves, especially the 16-18 group. If it's a separate number, the PM hours restriction may be relaxed; if it's the same number, the same rules apply.

Fights among the kids about phone use are reasons for a family meeting and some negotiation. Write down the agreement.

Too much time on the phone should usually be dealt with by doing nothing first. Leave them alone. Kids are supposed to spend a lot of time on the phone! It's good for them!! If it is seriously interfering with other family members' use of the phone, or the child is doing poorly in school, then advice, negotiation, or even Minor consequences would be appropriate.

Sex

As with drugs, you should first educate yourself about sex, sexually transmitted diseases, and birth control. Then try to find out how much your son or daughter knows. If they say, "Oh, Dad, I know all that stuff," give them "The Sex Test." Ask them to define certain terms, like orgasm, erection, lubrication, gonorrhea, foam, etc. Try to keep a straight face while you hear their definitions, and try to keep the lines of communication open. Be sure to listen first.

Here, also, you have less and less control over what they do as they get older. Try to discover what their values are about sexual involvement, then by all means, tell them yours. You may still be stuck with some unsettling differences.

Sibling rivalry

Extremely aggravating and persistent. No cure. After arguing, this is the next biggest problem parents of adolescents complain about in their children.

Involvement here is optional at any age, if you can stand the racket. Remember this is sort of a pastime for the kids, even though it can be a major aggravation for you. Also try to keep in mind the rule that says your level of anger about a problem is not always the measure of its seriousness. This may often be an MBA and you can tell them to work it out themselves. If you can't stand it and have to get involved (which most of us do), separating the combatants for 15-20 minutes in their rooms can work well. The child may choose a fine or some other consequence, but continuing the fight is treated as a Minor.

Remember: never ask what happened or who started it (absolutely the world's dumbest question) unless someone is physically hurt, and don't expect older children to be more mature than younger when it comes to household battles.

Smoking

Ideally, of course, no one should smoke, and active intervention should be used with the younger adolescents. Don't model it, first of all. If you insist on smoking don't do it at home, or just do it outside.

Then start with negotiating. Listen first! With 13-15 year olds, use the Major/Minor if they are smoking, but remember you have very little control over what they do outside of the house. Don't grill them—if you smell smoke on their breath, just impose the consequence—no yelling or lecturing.

For 16-18 year olds, drop the Major/Minor System, but insist they smoke only outside the house so the rest of the family are not "passive smokers." Smoking in the house is a Minor or Medium offense.

Swearing

If you're modeling the words you're telling your kids not to use, you've got a big problem. You can't very well tell teenagers not to use certain words when you are doing it in front of them. Some families set up a "swear jar" and just fine anyone, parents included, for bad language. Anyone who swears has to put 25 or 50 cents in the jar, and at the end of the week the money is donated to church or charity. This method seems to work well for many families, and the kids enjoy turning the tables on their parents occasionally.

If you don't swear yourself, a simple fine system that varies with the "badness" of the word may be the best idea. However, with the problem of swearing you may legitimately feel that you're fighting a losing battle, because the kids' friends and the movies usually model these words on a regular basis (this book is also a minor offender). Though you can't control what the teens do outside of your home, you can have some say about how they talk when they're with you.

Behavioral trouble at school

Behavioral problems at school, such as disrupting class, cutting, and smoking in the washrooms, require your involvement in the younger adolescent group. The Major/Minor System can be used if it doesn't involve too much double jeopardy (punishing after the school already has). With average or competent kids in the older group, these problems are not likely to be chronic or severe, so for first time offenses you may just use a little advice.

With problem kids, school behavior is often part of the problem, and a professional evaluation and counseling may be warranted. What if that's already been done and it didn't do any good? You could try to find a different therapist, or you may be stuck with crossing your fingers and avoiding the Four Cardinal Sins.

Using your things

Kids borrow clothes, misplace tools, and use up your makeup, deodorant, and shampoo. They also like your glasses, wristbands, jogging shoes, diet pop, and pens. This usually is not a big deal, so in many cases some friendly consultation may be adequate. Why not consider it a compliment—the little creatures are identifying with you! Nagging and screaming do no good at all.

How "Awful" is it, really? Rate it 0-100 on the Awful Scale.

If you have a chronic problem, try to negotiate some kind of deal or simply outlaw using your stuff. Violations, however, may take you to the Major/Minor System—simple fines are usually sufficient.

If all else fails, borrow some of their stuff.

Vacations: kids stay home

If you want to take a vacation and leave the kids home, and you just saw the movie *Risky Business*, what should you do?

"We don't need a sitter—what do you think we are, babies!?" That's what they'll tell you.

With 13-15 year olds, you get a sitter—an adult or college student. With competent or even average 16-18 year olds, you can consider leaving them. Be sure you negotiate things like locking up, use of cars, and—most importantly—friends over. Either no friends over while you're gone, or a limit of 1 or 2 reliable teens.

What about sibling rivalry while you're gone? That's their problem, provided no one gets hurt.

Stay in touch.

Work

Getting and holding down a job is an excellent experience for teenagers. Teens with jobs have their own money and learn something about responsibility, supervision, and getting along with others. It can also help them with getting out of bed in the morning during the summer.

If they have problems at work, you should stay out of it if you can, though active listening and lots of positive reinforcement are helpful. If they are looking for a job, don't nag them about it. You may circle job ads in the newspaper, if the teen doesn't find this irritating.

Occasionally a supervisor will call you about a problem your adolescent is having on the job. It's a good idea to try to stay out of the middle. If you can, tell your son or daughter who called, what they called about, and then ask your teenager how they think they will handle things.

It's usually preferable if the kids manage their own money. If the child goes through money like water, perhaps you can negotiate a way for them to regularly bank part of their paycheck.

Your Game Plan

Now you are ready to put together a strategy for dealing with your own children, right? After reading the suggestions in this chapter, consider the following:

1. Pick the three biggest problems you have with your teen. Are any of them MBAs?
2. Review the three ratings that you gave to your child, your relationship, and yourself.
3. Look at the recommendations in *Surviving Your Adolescents* for the three problems you chose.
4. Decide what is the best thing to do for each problem.

Before you do begin, you might want to check out, in the next chapter, some of the experiences other parents have had in using the ideas here.

Good luck!

16

SYA in Action

Let's go through a few hypothetical examples to get a better idea of exactly how parents might apply some of the ideas we have discussed. For each example we'll state what the problem is, what kind of situation we have (child, relationship, and parents' General Stress Index), and then describe and evaluate how the problem was handled.

Problem: smoking
17 year old: 5, competent
Relationship: 4, good, with Mother, 2 with Father
Parents' GSI: Mother 4, Father 3

Damon is smoking between one half and a whole pack of cigarettes per day. His parents are aware of this, because he sometimes smokes at home in his room or when other people aren't home. His father used to smoke until three years ago; his mother never did. Damon claims his smoking doesn't bother him, and that he finds it relaxing.

Damon's parents have talked to him about his smoking, and there have been a few arguments. Mom has pointed out the obvious health hazards. Dad has described to his son how he himself stopped. Damon has listened, and he has even acknowledged the value of some of their points, but has not altered his habit.

After reading *SYA*, Mom and Dad decide they will have one attempt at negotiating. They feel there are two problems: Damon's smoking being a hazard to himself and the passive smoking by other family members. They decide that for the first problem they will attempt to negotiate, and if that doesn't work, they will then keep quiet and Grin and Bear It.

For the second problem, however, the parents decide that Damon shouldn't be allowed to impose his smoke on the rest of the household. So if talking doesn't work, they will use the Major/Minor System if necessary.

Because Mom has the better relationship, she asks Damon if they can go out for ice cream or yogurt some night to discuss the problem. Damon loves yogurt. He agrees. Damon does not want to stop smoking, but he agrees not to smoke anymore in the house, provided that both mother and father get off his back about the problem. Mom agrees to communicate this idea to her husband.

Comment: Mom and Dad did very well. The good relationship Mom had with her son made things a lot easier. The parents' conference with each other before doing anything was also an excellent idea, especially since Dad and Damon don't get along too well, and they run the risk of only arguing.

Follow-up here will be very important. Will Damon be able to not smoke in the house at all, or will there need to be another negotiation or consequences if he can't? Will Mom and Dad be able to be quiet?

Problems: bedtime and homework
15 year old: 3, average
Relationship: 3, average, with Mother
Parent's (single) GSI: 3, average

Dynna is a sophomore in high school. Her grades are generally C's, though her mother and her counselor feel she is smarter than that. She usually stays up at night reading novels unrelated to school, and doesn't go to sleep until about 12:30 or 1 AM. In the morning she is often somewhat irritable, and has said she sometimes almost falls asleep in class. Mrs. Phillips rightly feels that her daughter's lack of sleep is hurting her emotionally as well as academically, but she doesn't quite know what to do about the whole problem.

It is 12:15 AM on a Wednesday in October. Dynna has a history test on Thursday which she hasn't studied for very much. Her returning from the kitchen wakes up her mother, who meets her in the hall outside her bedroom door.

"What are you doing?"

"I just went down to get something to eat."

"You should have been in bed a long time ago—don't you have
  a test tomorrow?"

"I was in bed."

"That's not the point. Those stupid romance novels aren't
  going to get you an A in history."

"At least they're more interesting than that bull——!"

"Listen to me! Fifteen long years on this earth doesn't give you
  the right to screw up your life. From now on, I want your
  lights out at 11 o'clock at the latest—you hear me!?"

"Of course, mother dear." (Slams door)

Comment: This is no good at all. Mom was, understandably, caught quite off guard on this particular night, which is partly why she makes three mistakes: 1) a spontaneous "problem solving" discussion, 2) no active listening before an attempt at a solution, and 3) a premature jump to the director role. Compliance here is not very likely, but further battles are in the offing. Mother's general stress level and the relationship, in addition, do not allow for a confrontation like this to be productive, especially when two problems—bedtime and homework—are being discussed at the same time.

What should Mom do? A little work on the relationship might help, then a brief attempt at consulting. If that doesn't work (it probably won't), it's on to negotiating, because the problem is important. Any future conversations, of course, should be planned in advance, especially when the relationship is only average. The incident above is a good example of the poor results that occur when problems are discussed on the spur of the moment.

Problems: arguing and use of car
16 year old: 4, average to competent
Relationship: 4 with Mother, 1 with Father
Parents' GSI: Mom 4, Dad 2

Beaver and his father are continually at it, primarily about one thing: the gas in the car. Beaver doesn't seem to realize that the needle can rise above 1/4. Dad does, because he's the one who is usually "filling the d—n thing up to the top," in addition to filling up his car and his wife's from time to time. This irritates him, and with good reason.

Dad naturally wants to explain a few things to Beaver about life, but the kid doesn't ever listen:

> "You use the car?"
> "Yeah."
> "How come there's no gas in it?"
> "There's gas in it."
> "Oh really. Wanna know how empty that tank is? If I threw a
>   match in it, nothing would happen!"
> "I'd like to see you try it."
> "OK, wise guy, now you listen to me..."

Comment: Another case of righteous indignation. How about a little active listening, Dad? No way. Beaver is certainly screwing up, but Dad is so far from being able to do active listening (Relationship 1, Dad's GSI 2) that it isn't funny. He and Beaver can just use each other for target practice, unless Mom steps in.

Mom and Dad should sit down together—without Beaver—and decide what to do. Mom then implements the plan and reports back to Dad. Things may be too far gone for any advice giving, so Mom might try negotiating a deal first. If that doesn't work, it's on to the Major/Minor.

Also, Dad needs to decide if he should address the issue with his son at all. If he does bring it up, it would be helpful if he asked himself if he's really trying to solve a problem or really trying to start a fight. It sounds so far like his true goal has been the latter, and it probably goes into areas other than car use.

Problem: sibling rivalry
15 year old: 3, average
Relationship: 3 with Mother, 5 with Father
Parents' GSI: Mother 3, Father 3

Jorge describes his little seven year old sister, Paula, as a total brat. The two of them can't seem to be in the same room without arguing. The fighting sometimes gets physical. Paula will then cry or scream and Mrs. Michael will run into the room to try to put out the fire. Though Jorge gets along better with his father, Dad travels a lot and is not around to handle most of the squabbles.

No amount of talking or arguing or lecturing has ever done any good. The kids just keep at it, and seem to almost consider it a pastime.

Finally, Mrs. Michael consults with her husband. They read *SYA*, then decide to do the following:

1. In most fights, they will discipline both kids; if the fight is bad enough, both children will be asked to go to their rooms for 10 or 15 minutes.
2. They will no longer ask what happened or who started it.
3. They will not expect Jorge, because he's older, to act more mature during an argument, though there will be increased consequences if he physically hurts his sister.
4. They will not expect the fighting to stop, realizing both kids enjoy it to some extent, but they will hope to cut down the frequency.

Mom talks to Paula, and Mom and Dad take Jorge out to dinner by himself. They discuss many things, including the new rules. Dad explains that— even though he can't be home all the time, he expects Jorge to follow the rules and his mother's instructions. If he doesn't, it will be back to negotiating, then Major/Minor if necessary.

Comment: Good thinking. Mr. and Mrs. Michael are using a version of the director role, since discussing sibling rivalry with the kids is often a waste of time. They are also being realistic in not expecting an older child to be more mature when it comes to fighting, and also in not expecting sibling rivalry to stop—ever.

Problem: drinking and pot
16 year old: 4, average to competent
Relationship: 3 to 4 with Mother (single parent)
Mother's GSI: 3

Triton has always been a pretty good kid, as far as Mrs. Tiegen is concerned, and he even seemed to survive the recent divorce fairly well. Lately, however, he has been "hanging" with a new crowd and staying out later. He also has been showing some signs associated with drug or alcohol use: uncharacteristic irritability, coming home and going straight to his room, a drop in grades, and what sometimes sounds like slurred speech when he talks to her over the phone when he's been out for a while.

Mrs. Tiegen has tried some advice, mentioning that she doesn't care for his friends too much, suggesting that sometime he invite them over for her to meet, and asking him directly if he is drinking or using other drugs. She has done a pretty good job of avoiding the Four Cardinal Sins, but she is getting more and more worried. In their conversations, Triton is usually pleasant but evasive, and if she pushes the talk he will become more irritable.

Mom decides to try talking things over, knowing she's unhappy with Triton's friends, grades, and hours. She tells him she would like to talk sometime, and suggests they go out for dinner. She is determined to start out by briefly stating her concerns, then she will use active listening to try to get more information.

Triton and his mother go to a drive in—his choice—and are sitting in the car after eating:

"You said there was something you wanted to ask me?"
"Yes, ah, I'm worried about how your doing. I think you've handled the divorce OK, but lately you seem to be different. Frankly, I'm wondering about your friends and about your drinking or using other drugs."
"Mom, give me a break!"
"That doesn't help me much."
"Well, what do you want to know?"
"I just told you what I'm worried about."

"Sure, I've had a few beers with the guys and smoked some
joints, but I don't see what the big deal is."

"You don't think it's any problem?"

"Hell, no—everyone tries it sometime."

"Well, I have to admit, I'm a little surprised—though maybe
I shouldn't be (a bit teary). Give me some time to think, and
maybe we can talk again, OK?"

"Whatever."

Comment: Mom is off to a good start with a difficult problem for her.
She has her thinking cap on, has done a good job of listening, cut off the
conversation when she got upset, and laid the groundwork for future talks.
She has not at all condoned what her son is doing, and may need to set
down some rules later, but her first job is to get reliable information about
what's going on and to establish a basis for talking.

Problem: bumming around
14 year old: 1, problem child
Relationship: 1 to 2 with Mother and Father
Parents' GSI: Mother 2, Father 2

Ramona has been having all kinds of difficulties for the past year or so. Her
parents aren't doing so well either, and sometimes it seems like—in this
family—no one gets along with anyone. It's Saturday and Ramona wants
to go bumming around at the mall, but Mrs. Rider may have other ideas:

"I'm heading off to the mall with some friends."

"Are you asking or just telling me? Don't just come waltzing
in here and inform me about what you think you're going
to do, young lady."

"All right. May I please wend my way, using extreme care, to
the shopping mall, with a few of my better behaved acquaintances, dearest mother?"

"Watch it, sweetie. I don't like the idea, go talk to your father."

"Talk to him yourself! I'm sick of this c—p!"

Comment: Nothing much is going right here. This is a clear instance where the parent and the adolescent have two totally different ideas about what role Mrs. Rider should have in relation to her daughter's desire to bum around. Ramona thinks that Mom should be in the observer only mode, and Mom seems to feel that she should be taking charge (she's correct, but didn't handle it well), and have the final say about whether or not her daughter goes at all.

Ramona has been having her problems lately, and if these have included difficulties while bumming around, then she shouldn't be going anywhere for a while. If she's been doing OK with this, in spite of her other difficulties, she should be allowed to go. If problems come up, the deal changes. Ramona says where she's going, with whom, and respects her hours. Mom doesn't grill her further.

Several months later. Mom decided she wasn't doing so well herself, so she went to see a therapist. Her husband was not interested in going. After several months of counseling, and also with the help of some antidepressant medication, she was feeling much better and thought it was time to deal with her daughter. At the suggestion of her therapist, she tried to sit down with her husband and discuss Ramona's problems, but he got upset and lapsed into his "She'd better shape up or else, god——it" routine.

Finding no help there, Mrs. Rider read _SYA_ and came to the conclusion that her relationship with her daughter was too bad for them to be able to do any kind of constructive talking, so she figured she'd better spend some time working on how they got along. Since her husband was a lost cause, the pressure was on her to try to do something. She decided on the safest route: asking Ramona to go with her to dinner and a movie. She knew her daughter would about faint with surprise, but Mom was ready and did her best to get into an active listening frame of mind:

> "Sometime, ah, you feel like just you and me going out to a
>   show, and then, ah, getting maybe something to eat after?"
> "Are you talking to me?"
> "Believe it or not."
> "You going nuts or something?"
> "Nope. Serious."
> "You gotta be kidding (laughs). You and me could never

agree on a movie in four godzillion years!"

"You pick."

"Folks, the lady has lost her mind! The butter has definitely
slipped off this woman's noodles."

"What show sounds good?"

"I got it—the old let's talk at Ramona routine. The litany of
past sins over a hot fudge. Dairy Queen psychotherapy. I'm
not interested. Nope. No thanks."

"I promise no talking about problems. I will not even once
mention your hair, but you have to do the same, OK?"

Comment: Three cheers for Mrs. Rider. She has truly shocked her
daughter, and she also showed, at least for the time being, that she is
doggedly determined to avoid war. Is Ramona weakening? She sounds
somewhat intrigued by her mother's weird new behavior, but she is
obviously very mistrustful of it.

This one's going to take a while.

Problems: money and loans
18 year old: 4, OK to competent
Relationship: 4 with Father
Parent's GSI: Father 3

"Dad, can I borrow $150?"

(Cough) "Sorry, musta been something I ate. What?"

"No, come on. There having a sale on these CD players,
and I'm short a little."

"Wait a minute. Didn't we give you your allowance a few days
ago? And what happened to your last paycheck—you can't
be out already?"

"I'm not out, I'm just low."

"Do you owe us any money now?"

"No, I'm all caught up."

"If I loan you the money, how do you want to pay it back?"

"With snakeskins. No, just kidding. With my paychecks. I
could give you $20 a week for seven or eight weeks."

"OK. You write out the deal on paper—it's a loan, not a gift, and I'll see what I can do about getting some cash."

Comment: Good example of negotiating. Dad doesn't get cranked out of shape by a spontaneous request, and also makes it clear what the deal will be with the money. The teen sounds like he's good for it.

Problem: depression?
15 year old: 3, average
Relationship: 3 to 4 with Mother
Parent's GSI: Mother 3

"Life sucks!"
"That's what I like about you, your constant good spirits."
"No, I'm serious."
"Well, why do you have to bother me about it?"
"Cause you're so easy to torture. No, I mean like things are a
   real b—h."
"Did something just happen to you?"
"Something isn't the word for it. You wanna know the @#$%
   that Wendy just pulled?"
"What?"
"Well, like, I'm at work—real busy—and she calls, and she's
   like...etc., etc."

Comment: Good recovery by Mom. It's amazing the child stuck around for it. It's time for some active listening; it may just be a bad day, rather than major depression.

And now one last thought before you get to work...

Part VI

The Future

17

Ten Years from Now

O ften when your adolescents are acting up it's easy to get quite worried about how these "kids" are going to turn out when they are adults. It may help you to keep several things in mind.

Straight Thinking II

Remember that adolescents are in the business of being different from you. Perhaps they even want to shock you from time to time. They have a lot of energy and want to try a lot of different things.

But even though they worry us from time to time, they are not yet the people they are capable of becoming. They are experimenting, changing, and learning. *For most of these kids, these changes will be positive in the long run.* In ten years you will not have the child you have today—you will most likely see an independent and responsible adult.

Supporting this idea are some interesting facts. One study, for example, found evidence to support the idea that periodic acting out behavior in your teenage years isn't all that bad, as long as you don't "O.D." on it. This research looked at three kinds of teens: those who used marijuana heavily, those who had only experimented with pot, and those

151

who had never tried it. These groups were then all evaluated on their overall emotional health using psychological tests and interview data.

What was found was that the kids who experimented with pot as adolescents were—when evaluated later—better emotionally adjusted than those who had either *never* tried anything or those who used marijuana *regularly*. This is not, of course, an endorsement for drug use, but it does suggest that the ones who experimented *learned something* from their experience.

Another interesting fact suggests that most adolescents are constructively learning about life during these transition years. Conduct disordered teenagers, as mentioned before, are a difficult crowd. The amazing fact, however, is that by the time they hit adulthood, more than 50% of them have reformed! They no longer act out like they used to. They also *learned a lesson*—often on their own without professional help.

If even CD kids can learn from their experimenting, fooling around, and getting in trouble during their adolescent years, it sure seems reasonable to expect that our average and competent teenagers are going to do an even better job of sorting out their lives. Did you ever learn something valuable from "activities" your parents never knew anything about?

Get Ready for the Future!

Along a different line, another interesting thought is that in ten years your 13 to 18 year olds will be 23 to 28 year olds! The vast majority of these men and women will be married, raising families, going to school, working, and living independently. Eventually, just about all of them will be just as much a part of our social fabric and work force as you are now. These 23 to 28 year old women also probably won't have partial crewcuts and orange hair, and their opposite sex peers may not be sporting large, colored, dangling earrings.

Finally, ten years—or less—from now something else could happen. You could become a grandparent! If the kids live close, you could actually have the opportunity to babysit your grandchildren frequently on the weekends!! Imagine chasing several two or three year olds around *your* house while *their* parents are relaxing at a motel over the weekend. Now let's see, where was it that we left that copy of *1-2-3 Magic*?